VIETNAM TRAVEL GUIDE 2025

Unravel the Mysteries of the Mekong Delta

Owen S. Vidal

Copyright © 2025.

All rights reserved. No part of this publication may be reproduced, distributed, or transmitted in any form or by any means, including photocopying, recording, or other electronic or mechanical methods, without the prior written permission of the publisher, except in the case of brief quotations embodied in critical reviews and certain other noncommercial uses permitted by copyright law.

Table of contents

Introduction
- Welcome to Vietnam
- Top Reasons to Visit Vietnam
- Brief History of Vietnam
- 1 week suggested itinerary
- Getting to Vietnam
- Exploring Vietnam

Major Cities
- Hanoi
- Ho Chi Minh City (Saigon)
- Da Nang
- Hoi An
- Hue
- Nha Trang
- Can Tho
- Ha Long
- Phu Quoc
- Da Lat
- Vung Tau
- Sapa
- Quy Nhon
- Hai Phong
- My Tho
- Pleiku

    Chau Doc
    Rach Gia
    Vinh
    Thai Nguyen
Cultural Experiences
    Museums and Art Galleries
    Temples and Pagodas
    Traditional Festivals
    Historical Sites and Landmarks
    Local Markets and Crafts
Culinary Delights
    Vietnamese Dishes to Try
    Top Restaurants and Eateries
    Street Food and Night Markets
    Cafés and Dessert Spots
    Food Festivals and Events
MUST SEE
    Nightlife and Entertainment
    Day Trips and Excursions
    Family-Friendly Activities
    Hidden Gems
Accommodation Options
    Luxury Hotels
    Budget Hotels and Hostels
    Boutique Hotels and Homestays

   Beach Resorts and Eco-Lodges
    Unique and Unusual Stays
Practical Information
   Currency and Banking
    Language Tips and Communication
    Health and Medical Services
   Safety Tips

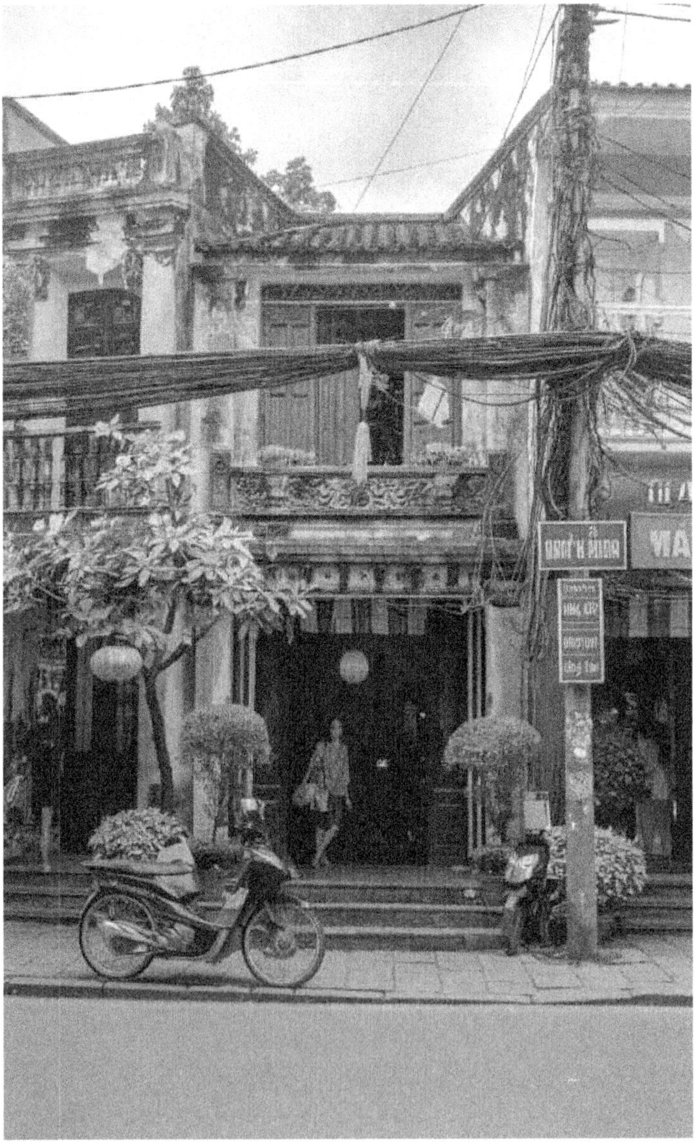

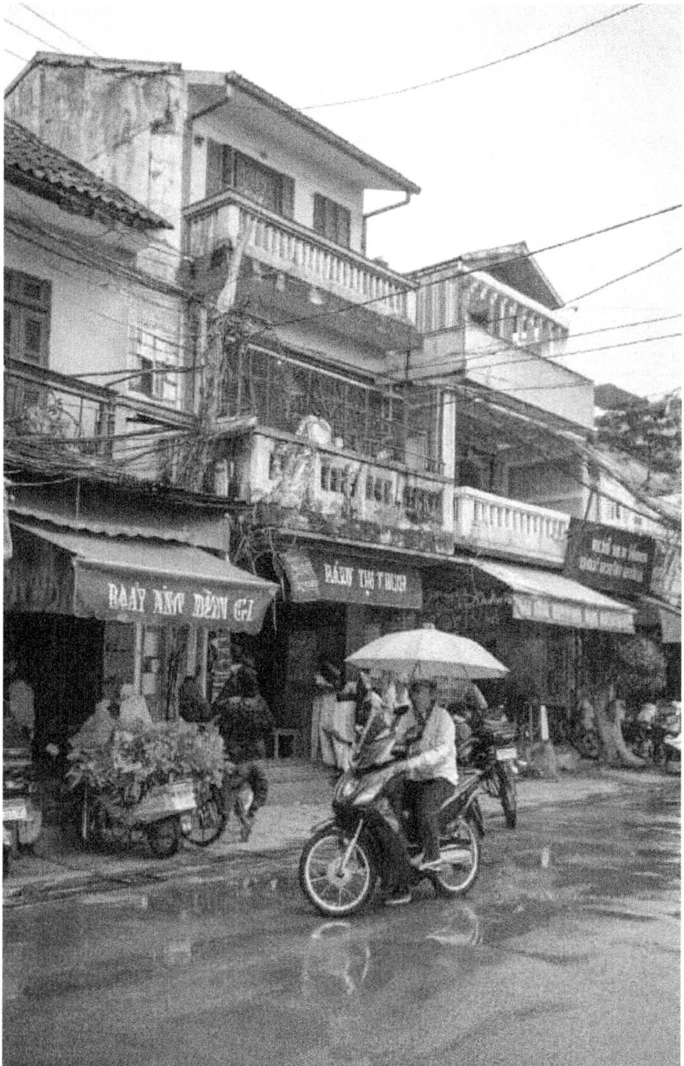

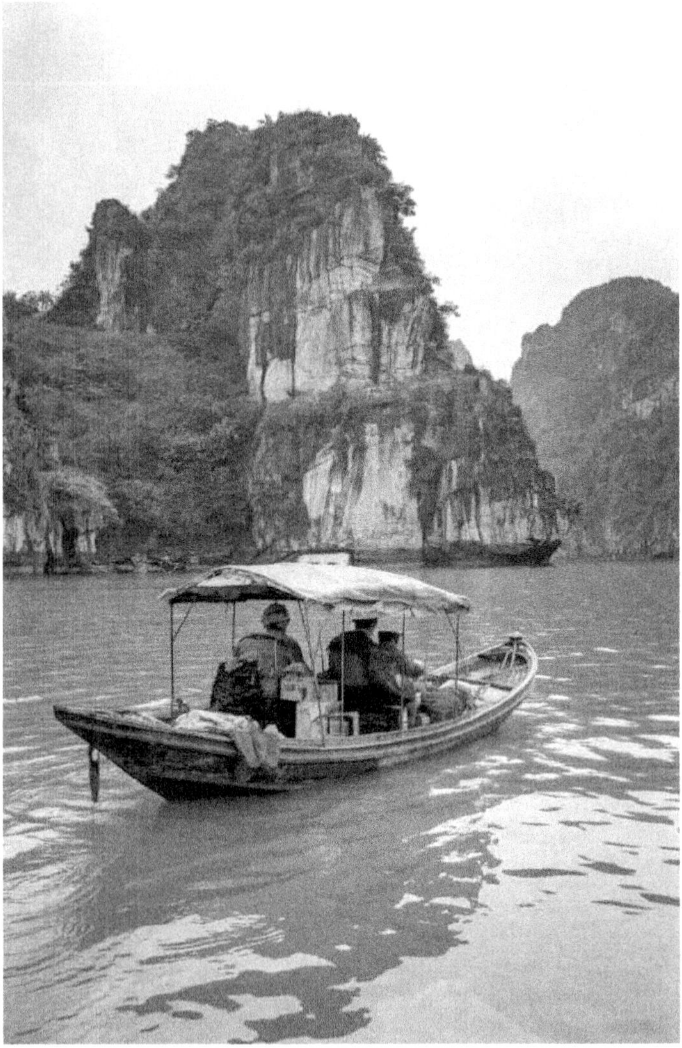

Introduction

Welcome to Vietnam

Vietnam wasn't just another trip. It was one of those places that sticks with you, not just because of the landscapes but because of the feeling it gives you. The kind that lingers long after you've left, making you wish you could press rewind.

I landed in Hanoi on a humid afternoon, stepping out into the controlled chaos of motorbikes, street vendors, and honking horns. The city felt alive in a way that was almost overwhelming, but within minutes, I found myself absorbed in it. There was no easing into Vietnam—it grabbed you and pulled you right into the action.

Walking through the Old Quarter, I felt like I had entered a different era. The buildings were worn but full of character, with narrow facades and wooden shutters that had likely seen more history than I ever would. Street food carts were parked at almost every corner, filling the air with a mix of aromas—grilled meats, fresh herbs, something sweet, something spicy. I wasn't planning to eat just yet, but that plan crumbled when I saw a lady squatting beside a low metal grill, flipping skewers of marinated pork. I sat on one of those tiny plastic stools that barely supported my weight and pointed at whatever looked good. The first bite of bún chả—grilled pork with vermicelli—was smoky, slightly charred, and packed with flavor. It was one of those meals that instantly sets the tone for a country.

The next morning, I took the long drive to Ha Long Bay. I'd seen the photos—those limestone karsts rising out of emerald water—but nothing quite prepared me for how surreal it looked in person. The boat glided through the bay, weaving between formations that seemed to materialize out of the mist. It was the kind of scene that makes you put your camera down just to take it all in. Later, I kayaked through some of the caves, the water eerily quiet except for the occasional sound of paddles hitting the surface. Somewhere in that silence, with towering cliffs above and dark caves ahead, I realized why people say Vietnam is magic.

Back in Hanoi, I stumbled upon something unexpected—Bia Hoi Junction. It was just a regular street corner, but by evening, it transformed into an open-air beer garden. Plastic chairs and tables spilled onto the road, and locals, expats, and travelers all sat shoulder to shoulder, drinking ridiculously cheap draft beer. It wasn't fancy, but that was the charm. I ended up sharing a table with a group of Vietnamese students, who were eager to practice their English. They taught me a few phrases, laughed at my pronunciation, and ordered snacks

I wouldn't have dared to try on my own. I still don't know exactly what I ate that night, but whatever it was, it went well with the beer.

From Hanoi, I took the overnight train to Da Nang. There was something nostalgic about train travel—the rhythmic clatter of wheels on tracks, the occasional glimpse of countryside through the window. By the time we arrived, I was already half in love with Vietnam.

Da Nang was quieter than Hanoi, but it had its own appeal. The beaches stretched endlessly, and the water was warm enough to swim in even at sunrise. But it was Hoi An that completely won me over. The lantern-lit streets, the yellow-walled shophouses, the scent of incense drifting from hidden temples—it felt like a dream. I rented a bicycle and got lost intentionally, pedaling past rice fields and stopping at random cafes. In one of them, an elderly woman served me the best bánh mì I'd ever had. The bread was crispy, the filling a perfect balance of meats, pickled vegetables, and chili. I told her it was the best, and she just laughed like she had heard it a hundred times before.

One night, I joined a local family for a home-cooked meal. It was part of a small tour, but it didn't feel touristy at all. They welcomed me like an old friend, handing me a plate and showing me how to wrap fresh spring rolls properly. We talked about life, about travel, about how food brings people together. It was one of those rare moments when you feel completely at home in a foreign country.

My final stop was Ho Chi Minh City, where the energy was turned up even higher. The streets felt wider, the traffic somehow even crazier, but there was a rhythm to it that made sense after a while. I visited the War Remnants Museum, which was heavy, necessary, and left me thinking about history in a way that no textbook ever had. I walked through Ben Thanh Market, where vendors called out in a mix of Vietnamese and broken English, convincing me to buy things I didn't need but wanted anyway.

On my last night, I sat on the rooftop of a bar in District 1, looking out at the skyline. The city stretched endlessly, neon lights reflecting off glass buildings, a mix of old and new. I thought about everything—the food, the people, the way Vietnam had made me feel alive in a way I hadn't expected.

Top Reasons to Visit Vietnam

Vietnam is one of those places that feels both familiar and full of surprises. From its buzzing cities to its tranquil countryside, there's a rhythm here that draws you in, making you feel at home while also offering something fresh at every turn. It's not just about the sights, though—Vietnam has a way of staying with you long after you've left. Here are a few reasons why this country should be on your list.

The food, without a doubt, is one of the top reasons to visit Vietnam. No matter where you go, you'll find something that surprises your taste buds. Whether it's the fragrant pho you slurp down for breakfast, the crispy spring rolls you nibble on in the afternoon, or the sizzling plates of barbecued meats served on street corners, every meal is an event. The beauty of Vietnamese food is in its simplicity, with fresh herbs and spices bringing out the natural flavors of ingredients. What's even better? It's affordable, making it easy to sample a wide variety of dishes without breaking the bank.

The landscapes are another thing that will keep you coming back to Vietnam. From the towering limestone cliffs of Ha Long Bay to the terraced rice fields of Sapa, there's no shortage of breathtaking scenery. If you're into hiking, the mountains around Sapa offer some of the best trekking experiences, where you can walk through villages, meet local tribes, and get a taste of life that feels far removed from the bustling cities. Meanwhile, Ha Long Bay, with its emerald waters and mysterious islands, is one of those places you have to see to believe. Whether you take a boat tour or kayak through hidden caves, it's a setting that almost feels like it's from another world.

But it's not just the natural beauty that sets Vietnam apart. The culture and history here are rich and deep, making it impossible to visit without learning something new. Cities like Hanoi are brimming with old-world charm, from the ancient temples to the narrow streets of the Old Quarter. Saigon (or Ho Chi Minh City) gives you a different perspective, mixing the old and new, where skyscrapers sit beside historic French colonial buildings. You can walk the streets and feel the pulse of a country that's modernizing rapidly, while also holding onto traditions that stretch back thousands of years.

The people of Vietnam are one of the highlights of any trip here. There's a warmth and friendliness that's hard to match, whether you're sharing a drink with a group of locals at a roadside bar or sitting down for a meal with a family in a remote village. The Vietnamese are proud of their heritage and eager to share it with visitors, whether it's through a conversation, a cooking class, or a walking tour. You'll quickly find that it's not just about sightseeing; it's about making connections that leave a lasting impression.

Lastly, Vietnam is incredibly affordable. From accommodation to transport, you'll find that it's one of the best value destinations in Southeast Asia. Street food costs next to nothing, and even in the more touristy spots, you'll still find plenty of budget-friendly options. The low cost of living makes it possible to travel longer, giving you more time to explore all that this fascinating country has to offer.

Brief History of Vietnam

Vietnam's history is a tale of resilience, adaptation, and a constant drive for independence. It dates back thousands of years, shaped by dynasties, foreign influences, and wars.

The early history of Vietnam saw the rise of the first Vietnamese civilization, the Văn Lang, around 2,000 BCE, under the rule of the Hùng Kings. This period marked the foundation of Vietnamese culture, particularly in the Red River Delta. Over time, the region was influenced by various neighboring cultures, including China, which exerted significant power over Vietnam for over a millennium.

In 938 CE, Vietnam's first major independence victory occurred under the leadership of General Ngô Quyền, who defeated Chinese forces at the Battle of Bạch Đằng River. This victory marked the beginning of a long history of Vietnamese resistance against foreign domination. For the next several centuries, Vietnam experienced cycles of internal division and reunification under different dynasties, such as the Lý, Trần, and Lê dynasties, during which Vietnam flourished culturally and economically.

In the 19th century, the French colonized Vietnam, along with Cambodia and Laos, forming French Indochina. This period marked a time of exploitation, as the French controlled much of the economy, resources, and political structure. However, this also sowed the seeds for the nationalist movements that would later lead to the struggle for independence.

By the mid-20th century, after years of resistance and the rise of communism, Vietnam was divided into two parts. The communist North, led by Ho Chi Minh, sought to unite the country under communist rule, while the South, supported by the United States, remained non-communist. The Vietnam War (1955-1975) was a brutal and devastating conflict that ended with the fall of Saigon and the reunification of Vietnam under communist control.

Post-war, Vietnam faced immense challenges as it rebuilt its economy and infrastructure, suffering from international sanctions and a centrally planned economy. However, beginning in the late 1980s, the country initiated economic reforms known as Đổi Mới, which shifted Vietnam toward a socialist-oriented market economy. This transformation spurred significant economic growth and development, positioning Vietnam as one of the fastest-growing economies in Asia today.

1 week suggested itinerary

Your adventure begins in Hanoi, the capital of Vietnam, where you'll arrive and check into your hotel. Spend the afternoon wandering through the Old Quarter, a bustling maze of narrow streets lined with shops, street food vendors, and colonial-era architecture. Make sure to stop by Hoan Kiem Lake, a peaceful spot in the heart of the city, and visit Ngoc Son Temple situated on a small island in the lake. In the evening, enjoy a bowl of pho at a local eatery, followed by a water puppet show at the Thang Long Water Puppet Theatre, which offers a glimpse into an ancient Vietnamese art form.

On the second day, dive deeper into Hanoi's history. Begin with a visit to the Ho Chi Minh Mausoleum and Museum to learn about the country's revolutionary leader, Ho Chi Minh. From there, continue to the One Pillar Pagoda and Presidential Palace, both significant historical sites. Afterward, head to the Temple of Literature, Vietnam's first university, and then spend time at the Museum of Ethnology, which provides a fascinating look at the various ethnic groups that make up Vietnam. In the evening, make sure to try some of Hanoi's street food, such as the famous egg coffee or a bánh mì sandwich.

On the third day, take a day trip to Ha Long Bay, a UNESCO World Heritage site known for its dramatic limestone karsts that rise steeply out of the emerald waters. Spend the day cruising around the bay on a boat, exploring caves, kayaking, and enjoying the stunning scenery. If you're lucky, you might even get to visit a fishing village and see how locals live and work. Return to Hanoi by evening, where you can relax and reflect on your unforgettable day.

The next day, travel south to Hue, Vietnam's ancient imperial capital. After arriving, start your exploration with a visit to the Imperial City, a vast complex of palaces, temples, and walls that once housed Vietnam's rulers. Spend the afternoon touring the Royal Tombs of the Nguyen emperors, such as the Tomb of Tu Duc and the Tomb of Khai Dinh, where you can learn more about the country's rich imperial history. End the day with a peaceful walk along the Perfume River, or perhaps take a boat ride to watch the sunset.

On the fifth day, head to Hoi An, a beautiful town known for its well-preserved Ancient Town, which is a UNESCO World Heritage site. The drive from Hue to Hoi An is scenic, with stops at the Marble Mountains along the way. Once in Hoi An, spend the afternoon wandering through the cobbled streets, admiring the old town's blend of colonial, Chinese, and Japanese influences. Visit landmarks such as the Japanese

Bridge and Tan Ky House, a traditional merchant's home. As night falls, the town comes alive with lanterns lighting up the streets. Enjoy a delicious dinner by the river and explore the bustling night market.

On day six, fly to Ho Chi Minh City, often referred to as Saigon, Vietnam's largest city. After checking into your hotel, begin your exploration by visiting the War Remnants Museum, which offers a sobering and insightful look into the Vietnam War. Next, make your way to iconic landmarks such as the Notre-Dame Cathedral, the Central Post Office, and Ben Thanh Market, where you can experience the vibrancy of the city and shop for local goods. In the evening, head to one of the city's rooftop bars for panoramic views of Saigon's skyline or venture to Bui Vien Street for a lively, colorful nightlife experience.

For your final day, take a day trip to the Mekong Delta, a region famous for its network of rivers, canals, and floating markets. Travel by boat through the delta's winding waterways, stopping at local villages where you can try fresh tropical fruits and watch artisans at work. Explore more of the delta by bike, or enjoy a peaceful boat ride along the canals. After an enriching day, return to Ho Chi Minh City for your last evening in Vietnam, perhaps indulging in fresh seafood or another delicious Vietnamese meal.

Getting to Vietnam

Getting to Vietnam is relatively straightforward, with plenty of international flight options connecting the country to major cities around the world. Vietnam has two main international airports—Noi Bai International Airport in Hanoi (the capital) and Tan Son Nhat International Airport in Ho Chi Minh City (Saigon), which are the busiest hubs in the country.

For travelers coming from North America, Europe, or other parts of Asia, connecting flights through major transit hubs such as Bangkok, Hong Kong, Singapore, or Kuala Lumpur are common. Many international airlines, including Vietnam Airlines, Cathay Pacific, Singapore Airlines, and Qatar Airways, offer direct or connecting flights to Vietnam.

If you're flying from nearby countries like China, Thailand, or Laos, flights to Vietnam are frequent, and the travel time is short—sometimes just an hour or two. Flights from Southeast Asia are typically budget-friendly, with low-cost carriers such as AirAsia and VietJet Air providing affordable options.

Once you land, getting from the airport to the city is relatively easy. Both Hanoi and Ho Chi Minh City have well-organized airport taxis, shuttle buses, and ride-hailing apps like Grab, which arc convenient and affordable options. For those traveling to other parts of the country, internal flights are available and efficient, with airlines such as VietJet Air and Bamboo Airways providing connections to cities like Da Nang, Hue, and Phu Quoc.

If you're traveling overland from neighboring countries, Vietnam has border crossings with China to the north, Laos to the west, and Cambodia to the southwest. Buses and trains are commonly used for these routes, though flights are generally quicker and more comfortable.
L

Exploring Vietnam

Exploring Vietnam is a journey that offers something for every kind of traveler. From the bustling streets of Hanoi to the tranquil beauty of Ha Long Bay, the fascinating history of Hue, the timeless charm of Hoi An, and the modern vibrancy of Ho Chi Minh City, there's no shortage of adventures waiting to unfold. The country's diverse landscapes and rich culture ensure that each destination offers its own unique experience.

Start your journey in Hanoi, where the blend of old and new creates a vibrant atmosphere. The streets of the Old Quarter buzz with energy, filled with motorbikes weaving in and out of traffic, vendors selling everything from fragrant flowers to fresh fruit, and historic buildings that tell the story of the city's colonial past. Here, you can lose yourself in the maze of alleys, finding cozy cafes, small boutiques, and street food stalls. Hanoi is famous for its pho, a noodle soup that you can enjoy for breakfast, lunch, or dinner, and its egg coffee, a sweet and creamy drink that locals swear by.

From Hanoi, a trip to Ha Long Bay is a must. This UNESCO World Heritage site is known for its emerald waters dotted with thousands of towering limestone islands and caves. You can take a cruise around the bay, swim in its calm waters, or simply relax on the deck, taking in the scenery. For those looking for a more active adventure, kayaking through caves or exploring floating villages will provide a unique view of the area. Whether you're aboard a traditional wooden boat or a luxury cruise, Ha Long Bay is an awe-inspiring destination that's hard to forget.

Next, head to Hue, the former imperial capital, where you can immerse yourself in Vietnam's royal history. The Imperial City, with its grand palaces, temples, and gardens, provides a glimpse into the past, while the nearby royal tombs are a testament to the country's long-standing dynasties. The Perfume River, which flows through the city, is ideal for boat rides, offering peaceful views of the surrounding countryside and historical landmarks. Hue is also known for its cuisine, especially dishes like bun bo Hue, a spicy beef noodle soup that's a local specialty.

Hoi An, a short distance from Hue, is a charming riverside town with a blend of Vietnamese, Chinese, and Japanese influences. Its Ancient Town is a UNESCO World Heritage site, with beautifully preserved buildings, lantern-lit streets, and a laid-back atmosphere. Here, you can stroll past silk shops, stop at the famous Japanese Bridge, or enjoy a meal at one of the many riverside cafes. Hoi An is also known for its tailor shops, where you can have custom clothes made in just a day or two. The town is a photographer's paradise, especially in the evening when the streets glow with colorful lanterns.

In Ho Chi Minh City (Saigon), Vietnam's largest city, the energy is palpable. From the historic Saigon Notre-Dame Cathedral to the bustling Ben Thanh Market, the city offers a mix of French colonial architecture, modern skyscrapers, and a lively street culture. Don't miss the War Remnants Museum, which provides a sobering but insightful look into the country's history. If you're a fan of street food, Saigon has a vibrant culinary scene, with pho, banh mi, and fresh spring rolls available at almost every corner. The city's nightlife is also something to experience, with rooftop bars offering stunning views of the skyline.

Vietnam is also a country of stunning natural beauty. The Mekong Delta, located in the south, is a network of rivers and canals that is home to floating markets, traditional villages, and lush greenery. You can explore the delta by boat, watching as local farmers work in the fields, or visit one of the many islands, each with its own charm. The delta is a peaceful contrast to the fast-paced life in the cities.

For those looking for outdoor adventures, the northern region of Vietnam offers opportunities for hiking in places like Sapa, where you can trek through terraced rice fields and meet indigenous hill tribes. The mountains here are breathtaking, with lush forests and dramatic views over the valleys below. There's also Phong Nha-Kẻ Bàng National Park, known for its caves, including the world's largest cave, Son Doong. Whether you're a seasoned trekker or a casual hiker, Vietnam's diverse landscapes offer something for everyone.

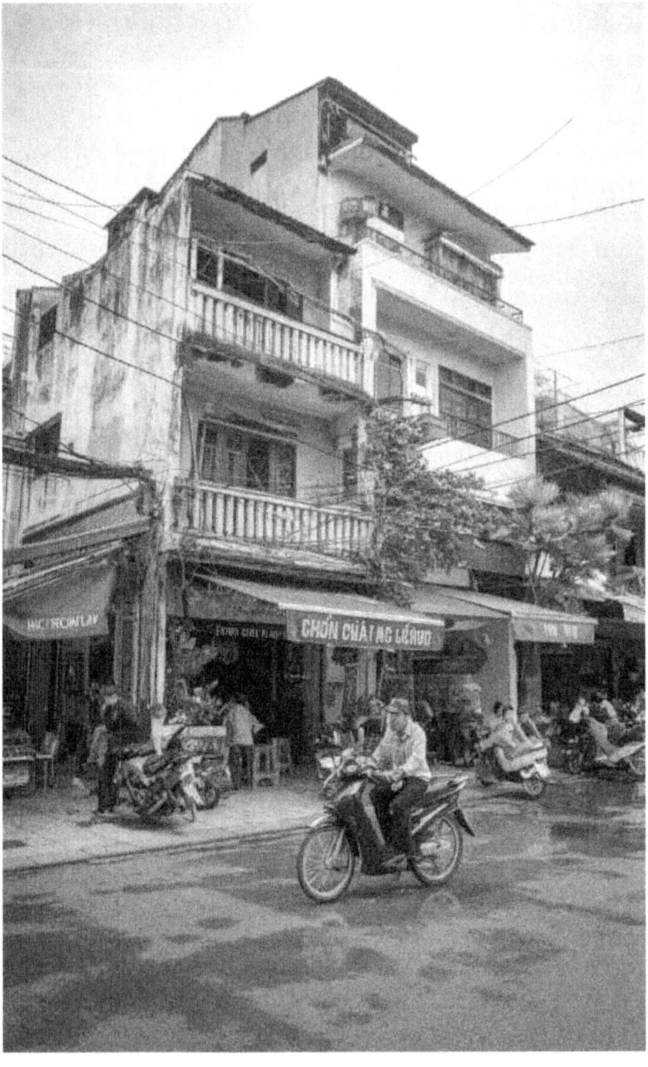

Major Cities

Hanoi

The Museum of Vietnamese History, located on the northern edge of Hoan Kiem Lake, is one of the most significant cultural institutions in Hanoi. This expansive museum presents an in-depth look at Vietnam's rich and complex past, from the Bronze Age to the present day. The museum is housed in a French colonial-era building that is itself a piece of history, with its grand facade and spacious interiors. It's here that you can explore a range of exhibits, including ancient artifacts, religious sculptures, and cultural displays that showcase Vietnam's diverse history and traditions. Notably, the museum features relics from the Dong Son culture, famous for its intricately crafted bronze drums, and a large collection of artifacts from the Vietnamese monarchy. The Museum of Vietnamese History is open every day from 8:00 AM to 5:00 PM, with an entrance fee of around 40,000 VND for foreigners. The museum is located at 1 Trang Tien Street, near Hoan Kiem Lake.

Another must-visit is the Vietnam Fine Arts Museum, which offers a comprehensive view of Vietnamese visual arts, from ancient sculptures to contemporary works. The museum, located in a beautiful colonial-style building on Pho Quang

Trung, has a vast collection that spans thousands of years, with exhibitions highlighting traditional folk art, Buddhist statues, lacquer paintings, and modernist masterpieces. The museum is divided into several sections, including galleries dedicated to the arts of Vietnam's different ethnic groups, contemporary art, and special exhibitions that change regularly. The museum's peaceful courtyard is a wonderful place to take a break from the hustle and bustle of Hanoi. It's open every day except Monday, from 8:30 AM to 5:00 PM. Admission costs around 40,000 VND for adults and 20,000 VND for students.

The Hoa Lo Prison Museum, also known as the "Hanoi Hilton," is a powerful site that takes visitors through a darker chapter of Vietnam's history. Originally built by the French in the late 19th century to hold political prisoners, the prison became notorious during the Vietnam War when American POWs, including Senator John McCain, were detained there. Today, the museum displays a variety of exhibits that explore the prison's role during both the French colonial era and the Vietnam War. The most striking section of the museum is the room dedicated to the treatment of prisoners, with detailed accounts and disturbing images from the era. Though the museum is a somber experience, it's an important visit for understanding Vietnam's complex past. The Hoa Lo Prison Museum is located at 1 Hoa Lo Street, and it's open daily from 8:00 AM to 5:00 PM. The entry fee is approximately 30,000 VND.

If you're interested in contemporary art, the Contemporary Art Centre is a great place to visit. Located in the heart of Hanoi, this gallery showcases the work of both Vietnamese and international artists. The centre often hosts temporary exhibitions, art talks, and workshops, making it a dynamic and interactive space for anyone with a passion for modern art. The exhibitions feature everything from painting and sculpture to photography and digital art, and the venue regularly hosts events that focus on new media and experimental art. The Contemporary Art Centre is located at 22 Hang Bai Street and is open from 9:00 AM to 6:00 PM. Admission fees vary depending on the exhibition, but it's usually around 40,000 VND for adults.

Hanoi's Museum of Ethnology, though a bit further out of the city center, is an essential stop for anyone wanting to gain a deeper understanding of Vietnam's 54 ethnic groups. The museum is beautifully laid out, with both indoor galleries and outdoor exhibits showcasing traditional houses, tools, and costumes. You'll find displays dedicated to the various minority groups, like the H'mong, Tay, and Khmer, offering insight into their customs, beliefs, and daily life. The museum is housed in a large modern building with spacious galleries, and it regularly hosts cultural events, performances, and workshops. The Museum of Ethnology is located at 1 Nguyen Van Huyen Street, Cau Giay District, and is open every day except Monday from 8:30 AM to 5:30 PM. The entry fee is 40,000 VND for adults and 20,000 VND for children.

Ho Chi Minh City (Saigon)

The War Remnants Museum in Ho Chi Minh City offers a deep and sobering look at the Vietnam War through the eyes of those who lived through it. Located on Vo Van Tan Street, this museum is a must-visit for anyone looking to understand the lasting impact of the war on Vietnam. The exhibits are both striking and emotional, filled with photographs, military equipment, and personal stories that provide an in-depth perspective on the war's brutality. One of the most moving sections is dedicated to the victims of Agent Orange, with harrowing images and accounts of those affected by the chemical defoliant used during the conflict. While the museum can be quite heavy, it's also educational, offering a chance to reflect on the resilience and strength of the Vietnamese people. The War Remnants Museum is open daily from 7:30 AM to 6:00 PM, with an entrance fee of 40,000 VND for adults and 10,000 VND for children. It's located at 28 Vo Van Tan Street in District 3.

For those interested in contemporary art, the Museum of Fine Arts on Pho Pho Duc Chinh Street is an excellent place to explore the evolution of Vietnamese art from the past century. The building itself is an architectural gem, a beautifully restored French colonial-era mansion that adds character to the experience. Inside, you'll find a range of works from various periods, from ancient sculptures and lacquer art to more modern pieces reflecting Vietnam's current social and political landscape. The museum also holds regular exhibitions showcasing contemporary Vietnamese artists, making it a great place to see how the country's art scene is evolving. The Museum of Fine Arts is open from 9:00 AM to 5:00 PM daily, and the entrance fee is 30,000 VND for adults.

The Ho Chi Minh City Museum, located in a grand colonial building that was once a mansion belonging to a wealthy merchant, offers a fascinating glimpse into the city's history. The museum's exhibits cover everything from the founding of Saigon to its rise as a major commercial center in Southeast Asia. Highlights include a stunning collection of maps and photographs detailing the city's transformation through French colonial rule and the Vietnam War. The museum also includes fascinating displays on the city's cultural heritage, featuring traditional clothing, religious artifacts, and displays on Saigon's role in the revolution. Open from 8:00 AM to

5:00 PM every day, the entrance fee is 30,000 VND for adults. It's located at 65 Ly Tu Trong Street in District 1.

A more recent addition to the city's art scene is the Contemporary Art Museum in the District 1 area. This museum highlights the work of both established and emerging Vietnamese artists, showcasing an array of contemporary pieces from various mediums, including painting, sculpture, and photography. What makes the Contemporary Art Museum stand out is its focus on experimental art, with exhibitions that challenge conventional boundaries and often explore social and political issues. It's a place that offers something fresh, with rotating exhibitions that keep the experience dynamic. The museum is open from 9:00 AM to 6:00 PM, with an entrance fee of 50,000 VND. You'll find it at 79A Le Van Tam Street, District 1.

If you're looking for a quieter, more introspective experience, head to the Fine Arts Gallery of the University of Fine Arts. This smaller, more intimate gallery gives you a glimpse into the work of up-and-coming artists from the university's faculty and students. The gallery offers a range of contemporary works, often with a focus on Vietnam's evolving cultural identity. The art here reflects the country's current artistic and social climate, and the exhibitions often feature experimental, thought-provoking pieces. The Fine Arts

Gallery is open Monday to Friday from 9:00 AM to 5:00 PM, and entry is free. It's located at 5 Phan Dang Luu Street, in Phu Nhuan District.

Da Nang

The Da Nang Museum of Cham Sculpture is one of the city's standout attractions and offers a captivating journey into Vietnam's ancient past. Situated at 2 September Street, this museum is home to the world's largest collection of Cham art, dating back to the Champa Kingdom that flourished between the 4th and 13th centuries. The museum's collection is both extensive and impressive, with over 300 artifacts, including intricately carved stone statues, reliefs, and ceramics. The museum provides insight into the Cham civilization's Hindu and Buddhist influences, with several sculptures depicting gods and goddesses from Indian mythology. Walking through the museum, you'll get a deeper appreciation for the artistry and culture of the Cham people, who once controlled much of central Vietnam. The Da Nang Museum of Cham Sculpture is open daily from 7:00 AM to 5:30 PM. Admission is 75,000 VND for adults and 20,000 VND for children. It's located at 02 2 Thang 9 Street, in the heart of Da Nang.

Another excellent stop is the Da Nang Fine Arts Museum, located at 78 Le Duan Street. This museum is dedicated to showcasing Vietnamese visual art, particularly works by local artists, and reflects the city's growing contemporary art scene. Inside, you'll find a variety of exhibitions, from traditional art forms like lacquer paintings to modern pieces in photography, sculpture, and multimedia. The museum also frequently hosts temporary exhibitions, offering a dynamic space for both emerging and established artists. The Da Nang Fine Arts Museum offers a quieter, more reflective art experience compared to some of the larger national institutions, with its intimate atmosphere and focus on Da Nang's own artistic talent. It's open daily from 8:00 AM to 5:00 PM, and the entry fee is just 30,000 VND.

For those interested in a more offbeat gallery experience, the Da Nang Art Museum on Tran Phu Street is worth visiting. The gallery offers an eclectic mix of contemporary art, with a focus on urban and experimental styles. It's a smaller space, but one that provides a platform for local artists to showcase their works in a modern setting. The gallery is known for hosting regular events and exhibitions that explore social and cultural themes, offering a fresh perspective on the region's artistic trends. The Da Nang Art Museum is open from 9:00 AM to 6:00 PM, and entry is free, making it an accessible stop for anyone interested in contemporary artistic expressions.

In addition to these museums and galleries, Da Nang also has a number of smaller cultural institutions, like the Ho Chi Minh Museum Da Nang Branch, which provides insights into the life of Vietnam's revolutionary leader. Located at 68 Ba Thang Hai Street, the museum contains artifacts from Ho Chi Minh's time in Da Nang and provides a deeper understanding of the city's role in the struggle for independence. It's open daily from 7:00 AM to 11:30 AM and 1:30 PM to 4:30 PM, with an entry fee of 20,000 VND.

Hoi An

The Museum of History and Culture in Hoi An is a small yet insightful stop for anyone interested in the town's fascinating past. Situated in the heart of Hoi An's Ancient Town, this museum is housed in a lovely, restored building that was once a merchant's house. It showcases the town's history, from its days as a busy trading port in the 15th century to its rich cultural exchanges with various foreign nations. The exhibits include ancient ceramics, historical maps, and artifacts from the different cultures that passed through Hoi An, including Chinese, Japanese, and European influences. The museum is open daily from 8:00 AM to 5:00 PM, and the entrance fee is 30,000 VND. You can find it at 10B Nguyen Hue Street, right in the heart of the UNESCO World Heritage-listed Ancient Town.

For a more hands-on cultural experience, head to the Hoi An Traditional Art Performance House, a cultural space that hosts daily performances of traditional Vietnamese music, dance, and folk art. This venue offers a deeper dive into the country's artistic traditions, with performances that often include iconic music played on traditional instruments such as the đàn tranh (zither) and đàn bầu (monochord). Visitors can also learn about Hoi An's unique cultural heritage through the shows, which explore the town's history and blend of influences. Located at 66 Bach Dang Street, the Hoi An Traditional Art Performance House is open every evening from 6:00 PM to 8:00 PM, and tickets usually cost around 100,000 VND.

Another spot worth visiting is the Museum of Folk Culture, located at 33 Nguyen Thai Hoc Street. This museum is dedicated to preserving the traditional crafts and customs of Hoi An, with exhibits showcasing the town's iconic lantern-making, silk weaving, and traditional embroidery. The museum also offers workshops where visitors can try their hand at these crafts, providing a unique, interactive experience that connects you to Hoi An's artistic legacy. The Museum of Folk Culture is open from 8:00 AM to 5:00 PM daily, and the entrance fee is 30,000 VND.

For art lovers, the Hoi An Art Gallery provides an intimate space to explore contemporary Vietnamese art. The gallery, located on Phan Chu Trinh Street, is a cozy, laid-back space that showcases works by local artists, with a focus on modern interpretations of Hoi An's culture and landscapes. From colorful oil paintings to intricate sketches and mixed-media pieces, the gallery is a great place to pick up a unique souvenir or simply enjoy the local artistic talent. Open from 9:00 AM to 9:00 PM, entry is free, though it's a good idea to purchase a piece of art as a way to support the local artists.

Finally, for those interested in Hoi An's maritime history, the Hoi An Maritime Museum is a hidden gem. This small museum provides an insight into the ancient maritime trade routes that passed through Hoi An, highlighting the role the town played as a bustling port in Southeast Asia. The exhibits include models of ancient ships, maps of historic trade routes, and tools used by local fishermen. It's a quiet spot to learn more about Hoi An's role as a commercial hub. The Hoi An Maritime Museum is located at 3 Nguyen Phuc Chu Street, open from 8:00 AM to 5:00 PM with an entry fee of 20,000 VND.

Hue

The Imperial City of Hue is a must-see when visiting this ancient city, offering an immersive experience into Vietnam's royal past. As a UNESCO World Heritage site, the Imperial City is an expansive complex of palaces, temples, gates, and gardens, all of which were once the seat of the Nguyen Dynasty. The Hue Imperial Museum, located within the Citadel, is where you can dive deeper into the history and treasures of this royal era. The museum houses artifacts from the Nguyen Dynasty, including ceremonial robes, ancient furniture, and jade ornaments, along with sculptures and pottery from earlier dynasties. The museum is open daily from 7:00 AM to 5:00 PM, with an entrance fee of 150,000 VND for adults. It's located inside the Imperial City at 1 Pho Duc Chinh Street.

For a more focused experience on the Nguyen Dynasty, the Royal Antiquities Museum is a smaller, quieter venue dedicated to the history of the imperial family. Located just outside the Citadel at 1 Tran Hung Dao Street, the museum showcases rare artifacts and artworks once owned by the emperors. You'll find collections of royal portraits, gold and silver objects, and ceremonial items used in the imperial court. The Royal Antiquities Museum offers a glimpse into the personal lives of the Nguyen emperors, with many items highlighting their tastes and daily rituals. The museum is open from 7:30 AM to 5:00 PM, and the entry fee is 30,000 VND.

The Museum of Royal Fine Arts is another spot in Hue that captures the essence of imperial art and culture. Located in a beautiful 19th-century French colonial-style building on Le Loi Street, this museum is home to an impressive collection of royal art, including lacquer paintings, porcelain, and intricate embroidery. The museum also offers exhibits on the construction of the royal palaces, giving visitors insight into the architectural and artistic achievements of the Nguyen Dynasty. Open daily from 8:00 AM to 5:00 PM, the entry fee is 40,000 VND for adults.

Another must-visit is the Hue Museum of History, where you can explore the broader historical context of Hue and its role in Vietnam's development. Situated in the city center, the museum contains exhibits on the origins of the city, its role in the Vietnam War, and the struggles faced during the French colonization. Historical relics, old photographs, and military artifacts provide a clear picture of Hue's significance over the centuries. The Hue Museum of History is open from 8:00 AM to 5:00 PM daily, with an entry fee of 40,000 VND. You'll find it at 23 23/8 Street.

If you're interested in the cultural traditions of Hue, don't miss the Traditional Craft Villages Museum, which showcases the city's renowned handicrafts. This museum celebrates the artisanship of the region, with displays of traditional wood carvings, pottery, silk weaving, and hat-making. It's an excellent place to understand the skills that have been passed down through generations and still thrive in the area. Located on the outskirts of the city at 10 Minh Mang Street, the museum is open from 8:00 AM to 5:00 PM, with an entry fee of 30,000 VND.

Nha Trang

Nha Trang, known for its stunning coastline and vibrant tourism scene, also has a number of museums and galleries that offer insight into the region's culture and history. One of the top spots to visit is the Nha Trang Museum of Oceanography, located on the scenic coastline at 1 Cau Da. This museum is perfect for anyone interested in marine life and the region's rich maritime history. The exhibits cover everything from the diverse sea creatures in the waters off Nha Trang to the scientific research conducted in the area. There are fascinating displays of fish species, giant whale skeletons, and models of traditional fishing boats, offering a window into the local fishing culture. The museum is open daily from 6:00 AM to 6:00 PM, and the entrance fee is

40,000 VND. It's an educational visit, especially for families or those curious about the local ocean ecosystem.

Another spot worth visiting is the Alexandre Yersin Museum, dedicated to the life and work of the Swiss-born French scientist who spent much of his life in Vietnam. The museum, located at 10 Tran Phu Street, celebrates Yersin's pioneering contributions to medicine, particularly his discovery of the plague bacillus and his work with the French colonial government. The museum houses personal belongings, photographs, and documents related to Yersin's time in Nha Trang, as well as his lasting impact on the medical community. The museum is open daily from 8:00 AM to 5:00 PM, and the entrance fee is 20,000 VND.

For art lovers, Nha Trang Art Gallery is a must-see. This gallery features a collection of works by local and national artists, showcasing a variety of mediums from paintings to sculptures. The gallery's collection often includes both traditional Vietnamese art and contemporary works that reflect the country's evolving artistic landscape. The Nha Trang Art Gallery provides a quiet space to admire the creativity that thrives in the area. The gallery is open daily from 8:00 AM to 6:00 PM, with free entry.

The National Oceanographic Museum of Vietnam is also located in Nha Trang, not far from the Museum of Oceanography. This institution offers an extensive collection focused on marine biodiversity, with interactive exhibits and live tanks displaying species found in the region. It's a great stop for those interested in marine conservation and understanding the relationship between Nha Trang's people and the sea. Open daily from 8:00 AM to 5:00 PM, the entry fee is 30,000 VND. It's located at 1 Cau Da, along the Nha Trang coastline.

Lastly, the Long Son Pagoda offers a cultural experience alongside a touch of history. While not a traditional museum, the pagoda itself is home to several interesting cultural displays, including a large Buddha statue and artifacts related to Buddhism in Vietnam. Situated on a hill, visitors can also enjoy panoramic views of Nha Trang. The pagoda is open daily, and entrance is free, though donations are appreciated.

Can Tho

Can Tho, located in the heart of the Mekong Delta, is a city that offers a fascinating blend of natural beauty and cultural history. While its charm lies largely in its floating markets and lush landscapes, there are a few museums and galleries that provide valuable insights into the region's heritage.

One of the most notable is the Can Tho Museum, located at 1 Hoa Binh Street. This museum offers an overview of the cultural and historical development of the Mekong Delta. The exhibits cover a wide range of topics, including the region's ancient history, colonial past, and the revolutionary struggle. There are displays of traditional Vietnamese clothing, agricultural tools, and historical relics from the local Khmer and Chinese communities. The museum also highlights the daily life of the people of Can Tho, giving visitors a deeper understanding of the local culture. It's open every day from 7:30 AM to 5:00 PM, and the entrance fee is 20,000 VND.

For those interested in the agricultural history of the region, the Mekong Delta Rice Museum offers a unique perspective. Located on Nguyen Thi Minh Khai Street, this museum celebrates the essential role that rice cultivation plays in the lives of people in the Mekong Delta. It houses various farming tools, models of rice fields, and exhibits on the rice production process, from planting to harvesting. The museum also includes a section on the traditional waterway transportation methods used by farmers in the region. The Mekong Delta Rice Museum is open daily from 8:00 AM to 5:00 PM, with an entrance fee of 15,000 VND. It's a great spot to learn more about the backbone of the region's economy and its agrarian traditions.

Art lovers visiting Can Tho will want to check out the Can Tho Fine Arts Museum, located at 13 Ly Tu Trong Street. This smaller gallery showcases a variety of works by local artists, many of whom focus on the life and landscapes of the Mekong Delta. The museum often hosts exhibitions featuring both traditional and modern art, providing visitors with a window into the creative scene of Can Tho and the broader Mekong Delta region. It's open from 9:00 AM to 5:00 PM daily, and entry is free.

Another highlight for those interested in local history and culture is the Ong Temple, located at 32 Hai Ba Trung Street. While not a typical museum, this historic Chinese temple provides insight into the Chinese community in Can Tho and their influence on the city. The temple, which has been beautifully preserved, features intricate wood carvings, religious artifacts, and statues of deities. It's a peaceful place to learn about the spiritual practices of the local Chinese population, and it's free to visit.

Ha Long

Ha Long, famous for its breathtaking seascapes and limestone karsts, is more than just a natural wonder. It also has a number of museums and cultural venues that offer insight into the region's history and the local way of life.

The Quang Ninh Museum is a prime destination for those wanting to dive deeper into the history and culture of Ha Long and the surrounding area. Located on 168 Ha Long Road, this museum offers an engaging look at the history, culture, and natural environment of Quang Ninh province. The museum features exhibits on everything from the ancient cultures that once inhabited the area to the development of Ha Long Bay as a modern tourist destination. The displays include artifacts from the prehistoric era, exhibits on local industries like coal mining and fishing, as well as artistic representations of the bay's natural beauty. The museum is open daily from 8:00 AM to 5:00 PM, and the entrance fee is around 30,000 VND. It's a great way to understand the cultural significance of the area beyond its famous scenery.

For those interested in the region's maritime history, the Ha Long Bay Museum is another excellent stop. Situated near the harbor, this museum focuses on the natural and cultural heritage of Ha Long Bay. It highlights the geological formation of the bay, which is home to more than 1,600 islands and islets. The exhibits include models of the bay's unique rock formations, historical photos, and displays on the aquatic life that thrives in the waters around Ha Long. The museum also educates visitors on conservation efforts in the area and the importance of preserving Ha Long Bay's delicate ecosystem. The Ha Long Bay Museum is open from 8:00 AM to 5:00 PM daily, with an entrance fee of 20,000 VND.

For art enthusiasts, the Ha Long Art Gallery offers a charming space to explore the works of local artists. This small gallery showcases paintings, sculptures, and photographs that capture the beauty of Ha Long Bay and the daily life of its inhabitants. The gallery often hosts rotating exhibitions, with a focus on both contemporary and traditional Vietnamese art. It's a peaceful spot to browse and perhaps purchase a souvenir to remember your time in Ha Long. The Ha Long Art Gallery is open from 9:00 AM to 6:00 PM, and entry is typically free.

Another unique venue in Ha Long is the Bai Tho Mountain Cultural and Historical Site, located near the center of the city. While not a traditional museum, this site offers panoramic views of Ha Long Bay and is a great place to learn about the history of the area. Bai Tho Mountain is historically significant, as it was a site where poets and scholars once gathered to compose poetry. Today, visitors can explore the mountain, view historical markers, and enjoy the view of the bay from the summit. The site is open daily from 7:00 AM to 6:00 PM, and there is a small fee to access the mountain.

Phu Quoc

Phu Quoc, known for its idyllicbeaches and crystal-clear waters, is also home to a few museums and galleries that provide insight into the island's history and culture. While its natural beauty often takes center stage, these cultural spots are well worth a visit for those looking to explore beyond the beaches.

The Coco Dive Center Museum is a unique stop for anyone interested in the marine life of Phu Quoc and the surrounding waters. Located in the Dương Đông area, this small museum offers displays on the diverse sea creatures that inhabit the waters around the island, along with information about coral reefs and marine conservation efforts. It also educates visitors on the environmental importance of protecting Phu Quoc's underwater ecosystems. It's not a traditional museum but more of an interactive space where visitors can learn about the area's biodiversity before heading out on diving or snorkeling excursions. The Coco Dive Center Museum is open daily from 8:00 AM to 5:00 PM, and entry is free, though you may be encouraged to book a dive or tour.

For those seeking to understand Phu Quoc's history, the Phu Quoc National Park Museum is a great option. The museum, located near the entrance to the national park, focuses on the island's rich biodiversity, indigenous plant life, and the history of the national park's creation. Visitors can explore exhibits about the flora and fauna of the island, including rare species of birds, plants, and animals. There's also a section dedicated to the preservation efforts that aim to maintain the natural beauty of the park. It's a peaceful spot, perfect for those who appreciate nature and want to learn more about the environmental efforts to protect the island. The Phu Quoc National Park Museum is open from 8:00 AM to 5:00 PM daily, with an entrance fee of around 30,000 VND.

Another interesting venue is the Dinh Cau Night Market Cultural Exhibit, located at the Dinh Cau Night Market in Duong Dong. While primarily a market, the cultural exhibit here provides an informal, interactive opportunity to learn about Phu Quoc's local culture and traditions. The display includes a variety of handcrafted items, local artwork, and information about the island's heritage, particularly its fishing communities and their ways of life. It's an excellent stop for those looking to understand the local customs and perhaps pick up a unique souvenir. The market is open in the evenings from 5:00 PM to 10:00 PM, and entry is free.

For art lovers, San Art Gallery is a small but charming space showcasing contemporary art inspired by Phu Quoc's landscapes and island life. The gallery features local artists, often focusing on works that highlight the island's natural beauty and vibrant culture. It's a great place to see how Phu Quoc's environment inspires creativity in its residents. San Art Gallery is open from 10:00 AM to 6:00 PM daily, and entry is free, though you may be tempted to purchase a piece to take home.

Da Lat

Da Lat, nestled in the Central Highlands of Vietnam, is a city renowned for its cool climate, lush landscapes, and French colonial architecture. While its natural beauty often takes the spotlight, the city also offers several museums and galleries that provide visitors with a deeper understanding of its cultural and historical background.

The Dalat Museum, located at 4 Phan Boi Chau Street, is one of the most important cultural institutions in the city. This museum showcases the rich history of Da Lat and the surrounding region, with exhibits covering the area's ethnic minorities, historical figures, and significant events. The museum's collection includes traditional costumes, agricultural tools, and artifacts related to Da Lat's colonial past, as well as displays on the city's founding and development. It's an excellent place to gain a deeper understanding of the area's cultural diversity and evolution. The Dalat Museum is open daily from 8:00 AM to 5:00 PM, and the entrance fee is 20,000 VND.

For those interested in Da Lat's French colonial influence, the Lam Dong Museum is another intriguing stop. Located at 1 Tran Phu Street, this museum focuses on the history of the Lam Dong region, where Da Lat is located. It offers exhibits on the indigenous ethnic groups, including the K'ho and Churu people, as well as displays on the French colonization of the area. The museum features historical documents, photographs, and artifacts that provide context to Da Lat's development as a resort town during the French colonial period. The Lam Dong Museum is open from 8:00 AM to 5:00 PM daily, with an entrance fee of 30,000 VND.

Art lovers will appreciate the Dalat Fine Arts Museum, located in a charming French colonial-style building on the outskirts of the city. The museum exhibits a range of contemporary Vietnamese art, including paintings, sculptures, and mixed-media pieces. Many of the works are inspired by Da Lat's natural beauty, with vibrant depictions of the region's forests, flowers, and lakes. The museum often hosts temporary exhibitions and offers a platform for local artists to showcase their work. Open daily from 8:00 AM to 6:00 PM, the Dalat Fine Arts Museum charges an entry fee of 20,000 VND.

For a unique experience, the Crazy House (Hang Nga Guesthouse), located at 03 Huynh Thuc Khang Street, doubles as an unconventional art space and an architectural wonder. Designed by Vietnamese architect Đặng Việt Nga, the building's surreal, organic forms have earned it a reputation as one of the most bizarre architectural landmarks in Vietnam. The structure is a maze of twisting corridors, tree-like supports, and whimsical rooms that resemble a fairy tale castle. While primarily a guesthouse, the Crazy House is also an exhibition of modern art and design. Entrance costs around 50,000 VND, and the house is open daily from 7:30 AM to 6:00 PM.

Another fascinating spot for those interested in Da Lat's history is the Bao Dai's Summer Palace. This former royal residence, located at 1 Trieu Viet Vuong Street, was once the summer retreat of Bao Dai, the last emperor of Vietnam. The palace is now a museum, showcasing the emperor's personal belongings, including furniture, photographs, and royal memorabilia. It offers a glimpse into the lifestyle of the Vietnamese monarchy during the French colonial era. The Bao Dai Summer Palace is open from 7:30 AM to 5:00 PM daily, with an entrance fee of 40,000 VND.

Vung Tau

Vung Tau, a coastal city known for its sweeping ocean views and laid-back atmosphere, also has a few museums and galleries that offer insight into its history, maritime heritage, and local culture. While most visitors come for the beaches, these cultural spots provide a deeper look into the city's past and artistic scene.

The Worldwide Arms Museum, located at 98 Tran Hung Dao Street, is one of the most unique museums in Vietnam. Established by a British collector, this museum features an extensive collection of military uniforms, weapons, and artifacts from different eras and countries. Walking through the museum, you'll see everything from medieval suits of armor to 19th-century muskets and modern firearms. The exhibits are well-organized, with detailed explanations in English, making it an interesting visit for history enthusiasts. The museum is open daily from 8:00 AM to 6:00 PM, with an entrance fee of 50,000 VND for adults and 25,000 VND for children.

For those interested in Vietnam's maritime history, the Vung Tau Lighthouse Museum, located near the iconic Vung Tau Lighthouse, offers a fascinating look at the city's naval past. The museum houses a collection of navigational instruments, old maps, and historical photographs that document the role of Vung Tau as a key port city. The museum also has exhibits on local fishing traditions, showing how the sea has shaped the lives of the people in the region. Open from 7:30 AM to 5:00 PM daily, the entrance fee is 20,000 VND.

The Vung Tau Museum, located at 4 Tran Phu Street, provides a broader historical perspective on the city. The exhibits cover everything from the early Cham civilization that once inhabited the region to the colonial era and the Vietnam War. The museum features relics from archaeological digs, old photographs of Vung Tau during the French occupation, and artifacts related to the fishing industry. It's a good place to learn about the city's transformation from a quiet fishing village to a popular beachside destination. The museum is open daily from 8:00 AM to 5:00 PM, with an entrance fee of 30,000 VND.

For a more artistic experience, the Vung Tau Fine Arts Gallery, located on Le Loi Street, showcases a collection of works by local and national artists. The gallery features paintings, sculptures, and mixed-media pieces that reflect the beauty of the coastline, the fishing culture, and contemporary interpretations of Vietnamese life. It's a peaceful space to explore and appreciate the creative talent in the region. The gallery is open from 9:00 AM to 6:00 PM daily, and entry is free.

A visit to Villa Blanche (Bach Dinh) is another cultural highlight in Vung Tau. This grand colonial mansion, built by the French in the early 20th century, once served as a retreat for French governors and later Vietnamese leaders. Today, it functions as a museum showcasing historical artifacts, including antique ceramics, imperial relics, and decorative items from Vietnam's royal past. The villa is perched on a hill, offering stunning views of the coastline, making it a great place to enjoy both history and scenery. It's open daily from 7:00 AM to 5:00 PM, with an entrance fee of 20,000 VND.

Sapa

Sapa, best known for its terraced rice fields and mist-covered mountains, is often seen as a place for trekking and cultural encounters with ethnic minorities. But beyond its stunning landscapes, Sapa has a few museums and cultural sites that offer insight into the region's history, traditions, and diverse communities.

The Sapa Culture Museum, located near the town center at 2 Fansipan Street, is the best place to start for anyone interested in learning about the ethnic minorities of northern Vietnam. This small but informative museum provides a well-organized look at the customs, crafts, and traditions of the H'mong, Dao, Tay, and Giay people, who have lived in the mountains of Sapa for centuries. The exhibits include traditional clothing, farming tools, and household objects, giving visitors a glimpse into daily life in the villages surrounding Sapa. The museum also explains the history of Sapa's development, from its early days as a French colonial hill station to the modern-day trekking hub it has become. Entry is free, and the museum is open daily from 8:00 AM to 5:00 PM.

For those looking for a more hands-on experience, the Sapa Art House, located on Muong Hoa Road, serves as both a gallery and a cultural space where local artists and artisans showcase their work. The gallery features paintings, textiles, and handicrafts inspired by the landscapes and traditions of Sapa's ethnic communities. The space also hosts workshops on traditional weaving and embroidery, where visitors can learn directly from local artisans. It's an excellent way to appreciate Sapa's artistic heritage while also supporting the local economy. The gallery is open daily from 9:00 AM to 6:00 PM, and entry is free.

Another cultural landmark worth visiting is the H'mong and Dao Cultural Exchange Center, which serves as both a museum and a meeting space for local ethnic groups to share their traditions with visitors. Located a short walk from the main market, the center offers live performances, craft demonstrations, and interactive storytelling sessions where visitors can learn about the myths and legends of the region. The center also sells handmade textiles and other handicrafts made by local women, providing a fair-trade option for those looking to take home an authentic souvenir. The cultural center is open from 8:30 AM to 5:30 PM, with a small entrance fee of 20,000 VND.

For a deeper dive into the region's ancient past, a visit to the Ancient Rock Field in Muong Hoa Valley offers a glimpse into Sapa's prehistoric history. Scattered across the valley floor, these mysterious carvings on large boulders date back thousands of years and remain largely unexplained. The site is often visited as part of a trek through Muong Hoa Valley, but for those interested in ancient civilizations, it's worth spending some time here to ponder their meaning. There is no official entrance fee, but local guides usually charge for a tour.

The Sapa Market, while not a museum, is another essential stop for those wanting to experience the living culture of Sapa. The market, which takes place daily in the town center, is a lively place where ethnic minority groups come to trade goods, sell handmade textiles, and showcase their traditional clothing. For those visiting on the weekend, the Bac Ha Market, located about three hours from Sapa, is one of the largest ethnic markets in Vietnam, drawing traders and buyers from all over the region.

Quy Nhon

Quy Nhon, a coastal city in central Vietnam, is best known for its quiet beaches, Cham ruins, and relaxed atmosphere. While it doesn't have as many museums and galleries as larger cities, there are still a few cultural sites that offer insight into its history, art, and maritime heritage.

The Binh Dinh Museum, located at 26 Nguyen Hue Street, is the best place to explore the history and culture of Quy Nhon and the surrounding province. The museum is divided into several sections, covering everything from ancient Cham artifacts to Vietnam's revolutionary struggles. One of the highlights is the collection of Cham sculptures, which date back to the period when this region was a stronghold of the Champa Kingdom. The museum also features exhibits on the French colonial era, the Vietnam War, and the development of Quy Nhon as a fishing and trading hub. It's open daily from 7:30 AM to 5:00 PM, with an entrance fee of 20,000 VND.

For those interested in ancient history, the Thap Doi Cham Towers, located on Tran Hung Dao Street, serve as an open-air museum of Cham architecture and culture. These twin towers, built between the 11th and 13th centuries, showcase the intricate craftsmanship of the Cham people, with their red brick structures, Hindu-style carvings, and decorative motifs. While the site itself is not a museum, it provides an up-close look at the artistic and religious influences of the Champa civilization. Entrance costs 15,000 VND, and the site is open from 7:00 AM to 6:00 PM.

Another fascinating site is the Long Khanh Pagoda, located in the city center at 141 Tran Cao Van Street. This historic Buddhist temple, built in the 18th century, is not only a religious site but also a place where visitors can appreciate Vietnamese Buddhist art. The pagoda is home to a towering statue of Buddha, as well as intricate wood carvings, calligraphy, and traditional Buddhist paintings. While entry is free, visitors are encouraged to dress respectfully and observe temple etiquette. It's open daily from 6:00 AM to 6:00 PM.

For a more contemporary artistic experience, the Quy Nhon Art Gallery, located near the beach on An Duong Vuong Street, showcases paintings and sculptures by local artists. The gallery focuses on works that reflect the landscapes, traditions, and daily life of the central Vietnamese coast. Many of the pieces capture the beauty of Quy Nhon's beaches, fishing villages, and Cham heritage. It's a small but worthwhile stop for those interested in Vietnam's modern art scene. Open from 9:00 AM to 6:00 PM, entry is free.

For a glimpse into Quy Nhon's maritime history, the Quy Nhon Fishing Museum, located in the port district, highlights the importance of fishing to the local economy. The museum features exhibits on traditional fishing techniques, ancient seafaring tools, and the life of fishermen in central Vietnam. Visitors can see models of fishing boats, learn about the region's seafood industry, and explore the traditions that have shaped Quy Nhon's coastal communities. Open daily from 8:00 AM to 5:00 PM, the entrance fee is 25,000 VND.

Hai Phong

Vietnam's third-largest city and one of its most important ports, is a place where history, industry, and coastal charm intersect. While it's often overshadowed by nearby destinations like Ha Long Bay, the city has a number of museums and cultural sites that offer insight into its maritime heritage, wartime history, and artistic contributions.

The Hai Phong Museum, located at 66 Điện Biên Phủ Street in the heart of the city, is the best place to start for an overview of Hai Phong's history. Housed in a beautiful French colonial building, the museum covers everything from the city's founding to its role in Vietnam's wars and its development as a major port. Exhibits include historical documents, photographs, and artifacts related to Hai Phong's resistance against French and American forces. There's also a section dedicated to the city's shipbuilding and trade history, reflecting its long-standing importance as a maritime hub. The museum is open daily from 8:00 AM to 5:00 PM, with an entrance fee of 20,000 VND.

For those interested in Vietnam's military history, the Hai Phong Naval Museum offers a fascinating look at the country's naval forces and their role in various conflicts. The museum contains ship models, naval uniforms, and historical accounts of battles fought in the waters around Vietnam. The outdoor section displays decommissioned military equipment, including torpedoes, cannons, and even a retired warship. The museum is located in the naval district near the port and is open from 8:00 AM to 4:30 PM. Entry is free, though some areas require special permission to visit.

A more unusual museum in Hai Phong is the Bao Dai Villa, a former residence of Vietnam's last emperor, Bao Dai. Located on a hill overlooking Do Son Beach, this villa-turned-museum offers a glimpse into the lavish lifestyle of the Vietnamese monarchy during the colonial era. The interiors remain decorated in a blend of French and traditional Vietnamese styles, with antique furniture, royal portraits, and historical artifacts. The villa also provides panoramic views of the coastline, making it as much a scenic stop as a cultural one.

It's open daily from 7:00 AM to 5:30 PM, with an entrance fee of 40,000 VND.

Art lovers should check out the Hai Phong Fine Arts Exhibition Hall, located at 19 Nguyễn Đức Cảnh Street. This gallery features contemporary works by local and national artists, with a focus on paintings and sculptures inspired by life in northern Vietnam. The exhibitions rotate regularly, often showcasing young and emerging artists alongside more established names. It's a quiet but inspiring space that highlights Hai Phong's creative side. The gallery is open from 9:00 AM to 6:00 PM, and entry is free.

For a cultural experience that combines history and spirituality, the Du Hang Pagoda is one of Hai Phong's most revered sites. Originally built in the 17th century, this Buddhist temple complex is home to beautiful wood carvings, intricate statues, and a peaceful courtyard filled with bonsai trees. While it's not a museum in the traditional sense, the pagoda is an important place to learn about the region's religious heritage. It's open daily from 6:00 AM to 6:00 PM, and there's no entrance fee, though donations are appreciated.

Another site worth visiting is the Hai Phong Opera House, a stunning French-built structure that stands as a symbol of the city's colonial past. While it primarily functions as a performance venue, the building itself is an architectural landmark and often hosts art exhibitions, traditional music performances, and cultural events. If you happen to be in town when a show is scheduled, it's worth attending to experience Vietnam's rich performing arts scene.

My Tho

My Tho, the gateway to the Mekong Delta, is a city rich in history, river life, and cultural traditions. While most visitors come for boat trips along the Tien River and the floating markets, the city also has a few museums and cultural sites that provide deeper insight into its heritage.

The Tien Giang Museum, located at 2 Le Loi Street, is the most comprehensive place to explore My Tho's history and the broader Tiền Giang province. Housed in a classic French colonial building, the museum covers the region's past, from its early days as a Khmer settlement to its transformation into a key Mekong Delta trading hub. The exhibits feature ancient artifacts, including pottery and tools from the Óc Eo culture, which flourished in southern Vietnam over a thousand years ago. There are also displays on the province's role in Vietnam's wars, showcasing military relics, photographs, and personal accounts of local resistance fighters. The museum is open daily from 8:00 AM to 5:00 PM, with an entrance fee of 20,000 VND.

For those interested in religious art and architecture, the Vinh Trang Pagoda is a must-visit. Built in the mid-19th century, this ornate Buddhist temple is one of the most significant in the Mekong Delta. The pagoda blends Vietnamese, Chinese, Khmer, and French influences, with intricate wood carvings, giant Buddha statues, and colorful tile mosaics. While it's an active place of worship, the temple also serves as an informal museum of Buddhist art and cultural heritage. Vinh Trang Pagoda is located at 60A Nguyen Trung Truc Street and is open daily from 7:00 AM to 5:30 PM. Entry is free, though donations are welcome.

The Dong Tam Snake Farm, about 10 kilometers from My Tho, is both a research center and a living museum dedicated to Vietnam's snake species. Established to study venomous snakes and develop anti-venom treatments, the farm also serves as an educational site where visitors can learn about the role of snakes in Vietnamese culture, medicine, and folklore. The farm is home to cobras, pythons, and other reptiles, as well as exhibits on traditional herbal medicine and snake-based remedies. Open daily from 7:00 AM to 5:00 PM, the entrance fee is 40,000 VND.

For a more local and interactive cultural experience, the Mekong River Craft Village near My Tho functions as both a museum of traditional handicrafts and a working artisan community. Here, visitors can watch skilled artisans making coconut candy, woven mats, and rice paper, all using techniques passed down for generations. The village offers hands-on experiences where visitors can try their hand at crafting, making it a more immersive way to engage with the culture of the Mekong Delta. Entry is typically included as part of a boat tour, but independent visitors can explore for free.

Another interesting stop is the My Tho Cathedral, a historic church that reflects the city's French colonial past. Built in the early 20th century, this Catholic church features European-style architecture with Vietnamese influences. Though not a museum, it provides insight into the religious diversity of the region and the lasting impact of colonial rule on My Tho's architecture and society. It's located at 32 Hung Vuong Street and is open for visitors throughout the day.

Pleiku

Pleiku, a city in Vietnam's Central Highlands, is often overlooked by travelers heading to more well-known destinations, but it has a rich history and deep cultural roots tied to the indigenous ethnic groups of the region. While the city itself is modernizing rapidly, its museums and cultural sites offer a window into the traditions of the Jarai and Bahnar people, as well as the region's wartime past.

The Gia Lai Museum, located on Tran Hung Dao Street, is the best place to start for anyone interested in the history and culture of Pleiku and the surrounding Gia Lai province. The museum houses a well-curated collection of exhibits detailing the lives of the Jarai and Bahnar people, including traditional clothing, farming tools, and religious artifacts. There are also sections dedicated to the region's history during the French colonial period and the Vietnam War, with military relics and photographs showcasing Pleiku's strategic importance during the conflict. The museum is open daily from 8:00 AM to 5:00 PM, and the entrance fee is 20,000 VND.

For those interested in indigenous architecture, the Jarai Rong House Exhibit, located within the museum grounds, provides an opportunity to see a traditional communal house up close. Rong houses, with their towering thatched roofs and intricate wooden carvings, are an essential part of the Jarai and Bahnar way of life, serving as gathering places for important village meetings and ceremonies. Visitors can explore the structure and learn about the symbolism behind its design, which reflects the spiritual beliefs of the highland communities.

Another significant site is the Camp Holloway Monument, a small but historically important landmark commemorating one of the most pivotal moments in the Vietnam War. Located just outside Pleiku, this site marks the location of a U.S. military helicopter base that was attacked in 1965, leading to a major escalation of American involvement in Vietnam. While there's not much left of the original base, the monument serves as a reminder of Pleiku's role in the conflict. There's no official entry fee, and visitors can stop by at any time.

For a more immersive experience of highland culture, a visit to a traditional Jarai village is highly recommended. Many villages around Pleiku, such as Plei Phun or Plei Bang, still maintain traditional lifestyles, with longhouses, wooden statues guarding gravesites, and animist rituals that are central to their spiritual beliefs. Some villages welcome visitors for cultural exchanges, where you can watch traditional gong performances, see how local handicrafts are made, and learn about the Jarai's matrilineal society. While there is no set entrance fee, it's respectful to visit with a local guide who can help facilitate interactions and ensure responsible tourism.

For art lovers, the Pleiku Contemporary Art Space, located near the city center, showcases paintings and sculptures by local artists, many of whom draw inspiration from the landscapes and indigenous cultures of the Central Highlands. The gallery features both traditional and modern works, making it a fascinating stop for those interested in how highland culture is evolving in the contemporary world. The gallery is open from 9:00 AM to 6:00 PM, and entry is free.

Chau Doc

Châu Đốc, a riverside town in the Mekong Delta near the Cambodian border, is known for its cultural diversity, vibrant markets, and spiritual sites. While most travelers pass through on their way to or from Cambodia, the city has a rich history and fascinating museums that showcase its unique blend of Vietnamese, Khmer, Chinese, and Cham influences.

The Châu Đốc Museum, located in the city center on Le Loi Street, is the best place to learn about the region's history and ethnic diversity. The museum houses exhibits on the Khmer and Cham communities that have lived in the Mekong Delta for centuries, as well as artifacts from the French colonial era and Vietnam's wars. You'll find traditional costumes, religious objects, and historical photographs that offer a deeper understanding of Châu Đốc's multicultural identity. The museum is open daily from 8:00 AM to 5:00 PM, and entry is free.

For those interested in the spiritual heritage of Châu Đốc, the Bà Chúa Xứ Temple is one of the most important pilgrimage sites in southern Vietnam. Located at the foot of Sam Mountain, this temple attracts thousands of worshippers each year, especially during the annual Bà Chúa Xứ Festival in April and May. The temple is dedicated to the Lady of the Realm, a deity believed to bring prosperity and protection. Inside, you'll find elaborate altars, intricate wood carvings, and incense-filled halls where locals pray for blessings. The temple is open daily from early morning until late at night, and entry is free.

Sam Mountain itself is a living museum of religious and cultural heritage, with numerous pagodas, shrines, and tombs scattered along its slopes. One of the most fascinating sites is the Tây An Pagoda, a striking mix of Vietnamese and Indian architectural styles. Built in the mid-19th century, the pagoda is known for its large Buddha statues, colorful towers, and peaceful atmosphere. It's open daily from sunrise to sunset, and there's no entrance fee.

For a glimpse into the daily life of the Cham people, a visit to a Cham village along the Hậu River is a must. The Cham, who are predominantly Muslim, have lived in this region for centuries, maintaining their distinct language, traditions, and crafts. The villages feature wooden stilt houses, mosques, and workshops where artisans weave beautiful silk and cotton textiles by hand. Many Cham communities welcome visitors, allowing you to learn about their customs and even try on traditional Cham clothing. There's no set entrance fee, but it's best to visit with a guide to ensure a respectful experience.

Another fascinating site is the Châu Giang Mosque, located in one of the Cham villages across the river from Châu Đốc. This mosque is an important religious center for the local Cham Muslim community and a beautiful example of Islamic architecture in Vietnam. Visitors are welcome outside of prayer times, and while there's no entrance fee, dressing modestly is recommended.

For those interested in local markets and trade, the Châu Đốc Floating Market offers a living museum of Mekong Delta commerce. Early in the morning, dozens of boats filled with fruits, vegetables, and seafood gather on the river, creating a vibrant and chaotic scene. The market is an essential part of life in Châu Đốc, reflecting the region's strong connection to the waterways.

Rach Gia

Rạch Giá, the capital of Kiên Giang province in Vietnam's Mekong Delta, is often seen as the gateway to Phú Quốc Island, but the city itself has a fascinating cultural and historical landscape worth exploring. While it doesn't have as many museums as larger cities, there are several places where visitors can learn about the history, traditions, and maritime heritage of this coastal region.

The Kiên Giang Museum, located on Nguyễn Công Trứ Street in the city center, is the best place to start. Housed in a classic French colonial building, the museum offers a comprehensive look at the history of Kiên Giang province, including its indigenous communities, Vietnamese settlers, and the impact of French and American conflicts. The exhibits include archaeological artifacts, traditional clothing, ancient to ols, and historical photographs showcasing the city's transformation from a small fishing settlement into a modern port. There's also a section dedicated to the Khmer and Chinese influences in the region, which are still evident in Rạch Giá today. The museum is open daily from 8:00 AM to 5:00 PM, and the entrance fee is 20,000 VND.

For a deeper understanding of the Khmer culture in Rạch Giá, the Tam Bảo Pagoda, located on Lê Hồng Phong Street, is an important religious and cultural site. Originally built in the 18th century, this Buddhist temple reflects a mix of Vietnamese and Khmer architectural styles. Inside, visitors can see intricate carvings, golden Buddha statues, and murals depicting Buddhist teachings. While not a formal museum, the pagoda serves as a living cultural center where locals come to pray and practice traditional ceremonies. It's open daily from 6:00 AM to 6:00 PM, and entry is free.

A visit to the Nguyễn Trung Trực Temple, located along the waterfront, offers insight into one of Vietnam's legendary historical figures. Nguyễn Trung Trực was a resistance leader who fought against French colonial forces in the 19th century, and he remains a revered national hero. The temple dedicated to him is an important pilgrimage site, with impressive architecture, traditional altars, and exhibits detailing his life and battles. The temple is particularly lively during the annual festival held in his honor in late September, attracting thousands of visitors from across the country. Open daily from 7:00 AM to 5:00 PM, the temple does not charge an entrance fee.

For those interested in maritime history, the Rạch Giá Fishing Port is like a living museum of the city's seafaring traditions.

This bustling port is the center of the local fishing industry, where visitors can see traditional wooden fishing boats, seafood markets, and daily life along the water. While there's no official museum, the port itself offers an authentic look at the importance of the sea to the people of Rạch Giá.

Art lovers should check out the Kiên Giang Fine Arts Exhibition Hall, a small but well-curated space showcasing the works of local and national artists. Located in the city center, the gallery features paintings, sculptures, and traditional crafts that highlight the culture and landscapes of the Mekong Delta. Exhibitions change regularly, making it a dynamic place to visit. The gallery is open from 9:00 AM to 6:00 PM, and entry is free.

For a glimpse into Rạch Giá's Chinese heritage, the Quan Đế Temple (Ong Temple) is worth a visit. Built by the city's Chinese community in the 19th century, this beautifully preserved temple is dedicated to Guan Yu, a legendary general in Chinese history. The temple's intricate wood carvings, incense-filled halls, and historic artifacts make it a fascinating cultural site. Open daily from 7:00 AM to 5:00 PM, there is no entrance fee.

Vinh

Vinh, the capital of Nghệ An province, is often overlooked by travelers heading to more famous destinations, but it has a deep historical and cultural significance, particularly as the birthplace of Vietnam's revolutionary leader, Ho Chi Minh. The city's museums and cultural sites provide valuable insight into both Vietnam's modern history and its rich local traditions.

The Ho Chi Minh Square and Museum, located in the heart of Vinh at 7 Ho Tung Mau Street, is the most important historical site in the city. Dedicated to Vietnam's most influential leader, the museum houses an extensive collection of artifacts, photographs, and documents detailing Ho Chi Minh's early life, revolutionary career, and contributions to Vietnamese independence. The square in front of the museum features a massive statue of Ho Chi Minh, making it a significant pilgrimage site for Vietnamese citizens. The museum is open daily from 7:30 AM to 5:00 PM, and entrance is free.

For a deeper exploration of Ho Chi Minh's roots, a short trip outside the city takes you to Kim Liên Village, his birthplace, about 15 kilometers from Vinh. This historical complex includes the simple thatched house where he was born, as well as a museum dedicated to his early life. Walking through the village, visitors can see how his humble beginnings shaped his revolutionary ideals. The site is open daily from 7:00 AM to 5:00 PM, with no entrance fee.

The Nghe An Museum, located at 4 Le Nin Avenue, provides a broader look at the history and culture of the Nghệ An region. The museum covers various periods, from ancient Vietnamese civilizations to French colonial rule and the American War. Highlights include archaeological relics, displays of traditional handicrafts, and exhibits on the role of Nghệ An in Vietnam's independence movements. It's an excellent place to understand how this province has influenced the country's history. The museum is open daily from 8:00 AM to 5:00 PM, and admission is 20,000 VND.

For those interested in religious and spiritual heritage, Cua Lo Temple, located near the Cua Lo Beach area, is a significant cultural site. The temple is dedicated to General Nguyễn Xí, a military leader from the 15th century who played a key role in Vietnam's resistance against Chinese invaders. The temple's architecture reflects traditional Vietnamese design, with elaborate carvings, incense-filled altars, and a peaceful courtyard. Open daily from 7:00 AM to 6:00 PM, the temple is free to visit.

Another important historical site is the Thanh Chuong Tea Hills, located about 40 kilometers from Vinh. While primarily a tea plantation, the site also serves as a cultural attraction, showcasing the agricultural traditions of the region. Visitors can take a boat ride through the picturesque tea fields, learn about tea cultivation, and sample fresh Vietnamese tea. The tea hills are open from 8:00 AM to 5:00 PM, and entry costs around 30,000 VND.

For those looking for an artistic experience, the Vinh Fine Arts Exhibition Hall offers a space for local and national artists to showcase their work. Located in the city center, the gallery features a mix of traditional and contemporary Vietnamese art, with paintings, sculptures, and installations that reflect the region's landscapes and cultural identity. Open from 9:00 AM to 6:00 PM, entry is free.

Thai Nguyen

Thái Nguyên, a city in northern Vietnam, is often associated with tea plantations and its role in Vietnam's revolutionary history. While it doesn't draw the same crowds as Hanoi or Ha Long Bay, the city has several museums and cultural sites that provide a deeper understanding of Vietnam's past, particularly in relation to the country's resistance movements and ethnic diversity.

The Museum of the Cultures of Vietnam's Ethnic Groups, located at 1 Đội Cấn Street, is the most important cultural site in Thái Nguyên. This museum provides an extensive look at Vietnam's 54 ethnic groups, showcasing their traditional costumes, musical instruments, farming tools, and religious artifacts. The exhibits are arranged by region, allowing visitors to see how different ethnic communities live, from the stilt houses of the Tây Nguyên highlands to the intricate brocade weaving of the Thai and Muong people. The outdoor section features reconstructed traditional houses, offering a hands-on experience of ethnic minority architecture. The museum is open daily from 8:00 AM to 5:00 PM, with an entrance fee of 40,000 VND for adults and 20,000 VND for students.

For history enthusiasts, the ATK Dinh Hoa Historical Site, located about 50 kilometers from Thái Nguyên, is one of the most significant revolutionary sites in northern Vietnam. This was the base of operations for Ho Chi Minh and the Viet Minh during the resistance against French colonial rule in the 1940s and 1950s. The site includes tunnels, bunkers, and simple wooden houses where key figures of the revolution lived and strategized. Walking through the complex, visitors can gain a deeper appreciation of the struggles faced by Vietnamese revolutionaries. The site is open from 7:30 AM to 5:00 PM daily, and entry is free.

For those interested in Thái Nguyên's renowned tea industry, a visit to the Tân Cương Tea Cultural Space offers a unique experience. Located about 13 kilometers from the city center, this tea museum and plantation highlight the history of Vietnamese tea cultivation, particularly the famous Tân Cương tea, which is considered one of the best green teas in Vietnam. Visitors can walk through lush tea fields, see the traditional methods of tea processing, and take part in tea-tasting sessions. The tea center is open from 8:00 AM to 5:00 PM daily, and entrance is free, though guided tea tours may have a small fee.

Another fascinating cultural spot is the Phủ Liễn Pagoda, one of the most important Buddhist sites in the region. Located on a hill overlooking the city, the pagoda dates back several centuries and features intricate wood carvings, bronze Buddha statues, and a peaceful courtyard. While not a formal museum, the pagoda provides insight into the religious traditions of northern Vietnam. Open daily from 6:00 AM to 6:00 PM, entry is free, though visitors are encouraged to make a donation.

Art lovers should check out the Thái Nguyên Fine Arts Exhibition Hall, a small but charming gallery that showcases contemporary works by local artists. The gallery features a mix of paintings, sculptures, and traditional crafts, often inspired by the landscapes and ethnic diversity of the region. Open from 9:00 AM to 6:00 PM daily, entry is free.

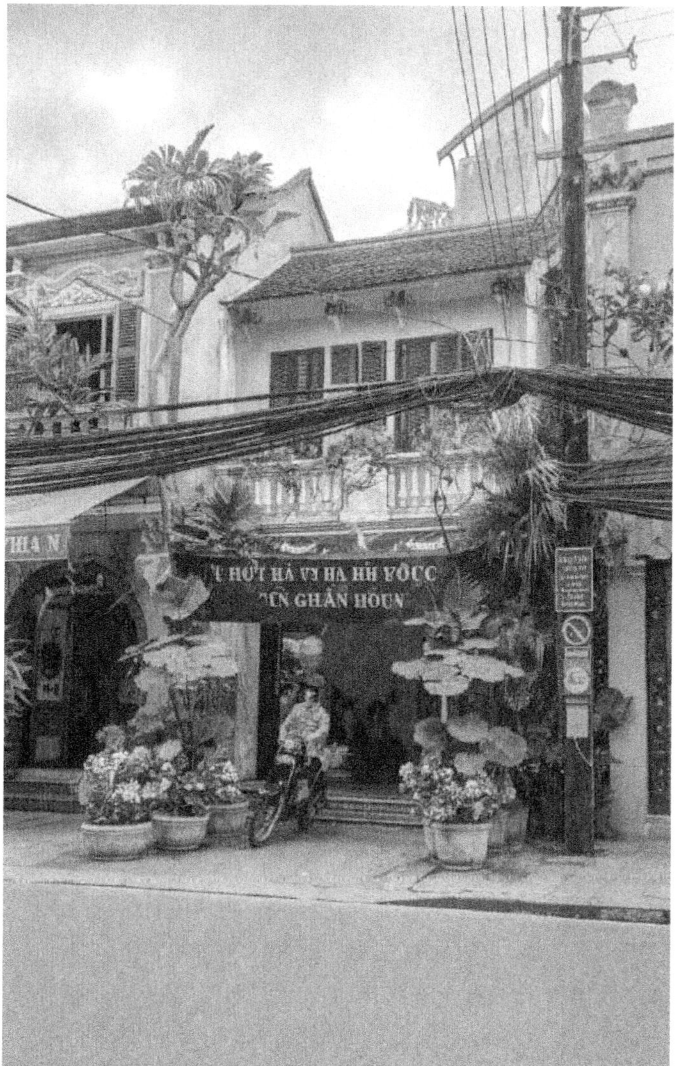

Cultural Experiences

Museums and Art Galleries

Vietnam's museums and art galleries offer an immersive look at the country's history, culture, and artistic evolution. From ancient artifacts to contemporary masterpieces, these institutions provide a deeper understanding of Vietnam's past, present, and creative expression. Whether you're interested in wartime history, ethnic heritage, or fine art, Vietnam has a diverse range of museums and galleries to explore.

Hanoi, Vietnam's capital, is home to some of the country's most significant museums and galleries. The Vietnam Museum of Ethnology on Nguyễn Văn Huyên Street is one of the best, showcasing the traditions of Vietnam's 54 ethnic groups through artifacts, costumes, and reconstructed village houses. Entry is 40,000 VND, and it's open from 8:30 AM to 5:30 PM. The Vietnam Fine Arts Museum on Nguyễn Thái Học Street is another must-visit, housing an impressive collection of traditional and contemporary art, including lacquer paintings, Buddhist sculptures, and folk art. Admission is 40,000 VND, open daily from 8:30 AM to 5:00 PM. For those interested in modern art, Manzi Art Space on Phan Huy Ích Street is a contemporary gallery featuring exhibitions by Vietnamese artists, while Work Room Four focuses on experimental and cutting-edge art.

Ho Chi Minh City has an equally rich selection of museums and galleries. The War Remnants Museum on Võ Văn Tần Street is one of the most visited museums in Vietnam, providing a powerful look at the Vietnam War through photographs, military equipment, and personal stories. Entry is 40,000 VND, and it's open from 7:30 AM to 6:00 PM. The Ho Chi Minh City Museum on Lý Tự Trọng Street offers an in-depth look at the city's colonial and wartime past, while the Fito Museum on Hoàng Dư Khương Street focuses on traditional Vietnamese medicine. For art lovers, the Ho Chi Minh City Fine Arts Museum on Phó Đức Chính Street is housed in a beautiful French colonial mansion and features works spanning centuries. Open from 8:00 AM to 5:00 PM, with an entrance fee of 30,000 VND, the museum's collection includes Vietnamese modernist paintings, folk art, and revolutionary-era pieces. The Factory Contemporary Arts Centre on Nguyễn Ư Dĩ Street is a leading contemporary art venue showcasing cutting-edge works from Vietnamese and international artists.

Da Nang, known for its beaches and bridges, also has a strong cultural scene. The Museum of Cham Sculpture on 2 Tháng 9 Street is one of the most important museums in central

Vietnam, displaying artifacts from the ancient Champa civilization, including Hindu-inspired stone carvings and temple remnants. Open daily from 7:00 AM to 5:30 PM, with an entrance fee of 75,000 VND. For contemporary art, the Da Nang Fine Arts Museum on Lê Duẩn Street features paintings and sculptures by local artists, many inspired by the region's coastal beauty. Open from 8:00 AM to 5:00 PM, with a small entrance fee.

Hoi An's Old Town itself is like an open-air museum, but it also has several dedicated cultural institutions. The Hoi An Museum of History and Culture on Nguyễn Huệ Street explores the town's development as a major trading port with artifacts from Vietnamese, Chinese, and Japanese influences. The Museum of Folk Culture on Nguyễn Thái Học Street focuses on traditional crafts, including lantern-making and silk weaving. Art lovers should visit Precious Heritage Art Gallery Museum on Phan Bội Châu Street, a fascinating exhibit by photographer Réhahn, showcasing portraits of Vietnam's ethnic minorities. The entry fee is 50,000 VND, and it's open from 8:00 AM to 6:00 PM.

As Vietnam's former imperial capital, Hue is home to the Hue Imperial Museum within the Citadel, displaying royal artifacts, ceremonial robes, and historical relics from the Nguyễn Dynasty. Open daily from 7:00 AM to 5:00 PM, with an entrance fee of 150,000 VND. The Hue Fine Arts Museum on Lê Lợi Street houses royal paintings, lacquerware, and traditional decorative arts from Vietnam's last ruling dynasty.

In Nha Trang, the National Oceanographic Museum in Cầu Đá is a standout, offering a deep dive into Vietnam's marine biodiversity, including preserved sea creatures and exhibits on ocean conservation. Entry is 40,000 VND, open from 6:00 AM to 6:00 PM. The Nha Trang Fine Arts Gallery near the beachfront showcases paintings and sculptures by local artists.

Can Tho, the heart of the Mekong Delta, is home to the Can Tho Museum on Hòa Bình Street, the largest museum in the region, covering the history of floating markets, Khmer and Cham communities, and traditional Mekong Delta agriculture. Open from 7:30 AM to 5:00 PM, with an entrance fee of 20,000 VND.

On Phu Quoc Island, the Coconut Tree Prison Museum provides a stark reminder of Vietnam's wartime past. This former prison site details the harsh conditions prisoners endured during the French colonial and Vietnam War periods. Open from 8:00 AM to 5:00 PM, entry is 30,000 VND. For a lighter cultural experience, the San Art Gallery showcases contemporary artworks inspired by island life.

Pleiku in the Central Highlands is home to the Gia Lai Museum, which explores the traditions of the Jarai and Bahnar ethnic groups. Exhibits include traditional stilt houses, gong performances, and ancient tools used by highland communities. Open daily from 8:00 AM to 5:00 PM, entry is 20,000 VND.

Chau Doc's cultural scene is shaped by its diverse communities. The Chau Doc Museum on Lê Lợi Street provides insight into the Mekong Delta's Khmer and Cham influences, while the nearby Chau Giang Mosque serves as an informal cultural center for learning about the Cham Muslim community in the region.

Rach Gia, the capital of Kiên Giang province, is home to the Kien Giang Museum on Nguyễn Công Trứ Street, which houses archaeological relics, traditional Khmer and Vietnamese artifacts, and exhibits on Rach Gia's fishing and trading history. Open from 8:00 AM to 5:00 PM, entry is 20,000 VND.

Vinh's Ho Chi Minh Museum and Memorial Complex in Kim Liên Village, about 15 kilometers from the city, is a major pilgrimage site dedicated to Vietnam's revolutionary leader. The complex includes his childhood home, a museum, and historical sites related to his early life. Open daily from 7:30 AM to 5:00 PM, entry is free.

Thai Nguyen is home to the Museum of the Cultures of Vietnam's Ethnic Groups, the most important museum in the north for understanding the traditions, clothing, and lifestyles of Vietnam's diverse ethnic communities. Open from 8:30 AM to 5:00 PM, entry is 40,000 VND.

Temples and Pagodas

Vietnam's temples and pagodas are more than just places of worship—they are living testaments to the country's spiritual traditions, history, and architectural beauty. Whether perched on mountain peaks, hidden in forests, or standing tall in the middle of bustling cities, these sacred sites offer a window into Vietnam's Buddhist, Taoist, Confucian, and folk religious heritage. From centuries-old structures with intricate carvings to modern temples that still attract pilgrims, each site carries its own story, blending faith, mythology, and history.

Hanoi, the spiritual and cultural heart of Vietnam, is home to some of the country's most iconic temples and pagodas. The Temple of Literature, built in 1070, is Vietnam's first national university and one of the best-preserved ancient sites in the capital. With its serene courtyards, stone steles engraved with the names of scholars, and traditional Vietnamese architecture, the temple remains a symbol of learning and wisdom. Not far from the city center, Tran Quoc Pagoda stands as the oldest pagoda in Hanoi. Located on a small island in West Lake, it dates back to the 6th century and is an important Buddhist site where locals come to pray, light incense, and seek blessings. Another must-visit is Ngoc Son Temple, situated on a small islet in Hoan Kiem Lake. Connected to the shore by the iconic red-painted bridge, this temple honors the legendary General Trần Hưng Đạo and is one of Hanoi's most visited landmarks.

Ho Chi Minh City, while modern and fast-paced, has its share of beautiful temples and pagodas that reflect its multicultural heritage. The Jade Emperor Pagoda, built in the early 20th century, is one of the most atmospheric places in the city. With its smoky incense, intricate wood carvings, and depictions of Taoist deities, the temple offers a fascinating glimpse into local spiritual practices. Vĩnh Nghiêm Pagoda, with its tall pagoda tower and peaceful gardens, is a more recent addition to the city's religious landscape but remains a significant site for Buddhist followers. Giac Lam Pagoda, the oldest in Ho Chi Minh City, dates back to the 18th century and features golden statues, traditional Buddhist altars, and a large Bodhi tree planted from a seed taken from the original tree in India under which the Buddha attained enlightenment.

Hue, the former imperial capital, is home to some of the most historically significant pagodas in Vietnam. The Thien Mu Pagoda, perched on a hill overlooking the Perfume River, is one of the most recognizable landmarks in the country. Its seven-story pagoda tower, called Phuoc Duyen, is an architectural masterpiece that has stood for centuries, while the peaceful gardens and Buddhist relics inside the temple complex offer insight into Vietnam's spiritual traditions. Another must-see is Tu Hieu Pagoda, hidden in a pine forest outside Hue. This temple is known for its connection to Zen Buddhism and was once home to the famous Buddhist monk Thich Nhat Hanh.

Hoi An, with its well-preserved ancient town, is home to several beautiful temples that blend Vietnamese, Chinese, and Japanese influences. Quan Cong Temple, dedicated to a Chinese general from the Three Kingdoms period, is one of the most vibrant, with elaborate red and gold interiors. The Fujian Assembly Hall, often mistaken for a temple, is another fascinating site, originally built as a gathering place for Chinese traders but now used for worshiping Thien Hau, the goddess of the sea. Chùa Cầu, or the Japanese Covered Bridge Pagoda, is a unique structure that serves both as a bridge and a small Buddhist shrine, making it one of Hoi An's most photographed spots.

Da Nang, often seen as a modern beach city, also has important spiritual sites. The Linh Ung Pagoda, located on Son Tra Peninsula, features Vietnam's tallest Lady Buddha statue, standing at 67 meters and overlooking the sea. This temple is a popular pilgrimage site and offers stunning panoramic views of the coastline. Further inland, the Marble Mountains house a series of cave pagodas, including Tam Thai Pagoda and Huyen Khong Cave, where Buddhist altars are carved into the stone walls, creating an otherworldly atmosphere.

In Ninh Binh, the Bai Dinh Pagoda Complex is the largest Buddhist temple complex in Vietnam. With its giant bronze Buddha statues, towering stupas, and intricate carvings, Bai Dinh attracts pilgrims and tourists alike. Nearby, Bích Động Pagoda, built into the limestone mountains, offers a more serene and mystical setting, accessible via a stone bridge leading to a series of ancient caves and shrines.

Tay Ninh, located near Ho Chi Minh City, is the spiritual home of Cao Dai Temple, the headquarters of Caodaism, a unique Vietnamese religion that blends Buddhism, Christianity, Taoism, and Confucianism. The temple is one of the most visually striking in Vietnam, with its colorful façade, dragon motifs, and a large eye symbol representing divine wisdom. Visitors are welcome to observe the daily prayer ceremonies, which are a fascinating blend of chanting, music, and symbolic rituals.

In the Mekong Delta, My Tho's Vinh Trang Pagoda is one of the most famous Buddhist temples in southern Vietnam. Built in the 19th century, this temple combines Vietnamese, Khmer, and European architectural styles, with towering Buddha statues, peaceful gardens, and intricately designed pillars.

Can Tho, the capital of the Mekong Delta, is home to Ong Pagoda, a colorful Chinese-style temple that reflects the influence of the Chinese community in the region. Dedicated to the god Quan Cong, this temple is always filled with the scent of burning incense and the flickering light of red lanterns.

Phu Quoc, known for its beaches, also has several spiritual sites, including Ho Quoc Pagoda, which overlooks the sea and offers a peaceful retreat away from the island's tourist crowds.

Traditional Festivals

Vietnam's traditional festivals are deeply rooted in history, legend, and the rhythms of rural life. Some mark the changing seasons, others honor historical figures or spirits, and many bring entire communities together in celebration. These festivals aren't just about ceremony; they're an expression of Vietnam's cultural identity, passed down for generations. Whether it's dragon dances, lantern-lit rivers, or incense-filled temple courtyards, each festival carries a story that reflects the beliefs and traditions of the people.

The most important celebration of the year is Tết Nguyên Đán, or Lunar New Year. More than just a new beginning, Tết is when families come together, honor their ancestors, and welcome good fortune. In the days leading up to the holiday, cities and villages transform. Streets fill with the scent of peach blossoms and kumquat trees, which symbolize prosperity. People clean their homes, settle debts, and prepare elaborate feasts. On New Year's Eve, firecrackers (banned in many places now, but still used in some areas) scare away bad luck, while families gather to watch the fireworks and share bánh chưng, a sticky rice cake wrapped in banana leaves. Tết isn't just about big cities like Hanoi and Ho Chi Minh City—some of the most heartfelt celebrations happen in the countryside, where locals hold village festivals with traditional games, dragon dances, and offerings to ancestors.

Another major event is the Mid-Autumn Festival, known locally as Tết Trung Thu. Originally a harvest festival, it has become a time for children, lanterns, and mooncakes. The full moon is said to be at its brightest and most beautiful during this time, and in towns like Hoi An, the streets glow with paper lanterns of every shape and color. Families prepare offerings to the moon, and children parade through the streets carrying star-shaped lanterns while lion dancers drum out a rhythmic beat. The atmosphere is lively, with people sharing mooncakes filled with lotus seed paste or salted egg yolks. Though it's a celebration for children, it holds a nostalgic charm for all ages.

In the north, one of the most vibrant spring festivals is the Perfume Pagoda Festival, held at one of Vietnam's most important Buddhist sites in the limestone mountains outside Hanoi. Every year, pilgrims travel by boat along the Yen River, then climb the stone steps to the Perfume Pagoda, believed to be a gateway to enlightenment. The journey is part of the experience, with boats drifting past rice paddies and karst cliffs before reaching the pagoda complex. People burn incense, make offerings, and pray for health and prosperity. It's a festival with a spiritual core, but also a social event, with vendors selling everything from religious amulets to grilled river fish.

The Hung Kings Temple Festival, held in Phu Tho province, pays tribute to the legendary Hung Kings, the founders of Vietnam. Every year in the third lunar month, thousands of people make the pilgrimage to the temple complex, where processions, music, and incense ceremonies take place. The atmosphere is electric, with martial arts displays, folk singing, and traditional games like wrestling and bamboo swings. The festival is as much about national pride as it is about honoring the past.

In Hue, the former imperial capital, the Hue Festival is a showcase of Vietnam's royal heritage, with reenactments of Nguyen Dynasty rituals, traditional music performances, and boat parades on the Perfume River. Held every two years, it draws artists and performers from across the country and beyond. The streets of Hue come alive with calligraphy exhibitions, lantern-lit processions, and theatrical performances that bring the city's history to life.

The Giong Festival, held just outside Hanoi, honors Saint Giong, a mythical warrior who rode an iron horse into battle to defeat foreign invaders. Every spring, locals reenact his legendary fight, complete with ceremonial offerings, drumming, and a dramatic procession where villagers in traditional costumes march through the streets. It's an event steeped in folklore, where history and myth blur together.

In southern Vietnam, the Ba Chua Xu Festival in Chau Doc is one of the biggest spiritual gatherings in the Mekong Delta. Devotees from across the region travel to Sam Mountain to pray at the temple of Ba Chua Xu, the "Lady of the Realm," believed to bring prosperity and protection. The festival involves elaborate rituals, including the ceremonial bathing of her statue, traditional dances, and theatrical performances that recount her legend. It's a blend of Buddhism, folk beliefs, and local tradition, drawing tens of thousands of worshippers.

On the coast, the Whale Worship Festival is celebrated in fishing villages from Da Nang to Vung Tau. Fishermen believe whales are sacred guardians who protect them at sea, and each year, they hold a festival in their honor. Offerings of food and incense are made at local temples, while processions carry ornate whale effigies through the streets. The festival is filled with boat races, lion dances, and prayers for calm seas and bountiful catches.

Historical Sites and Landmarks

Vietnam's history is etched into its cities, mountains, and coastline. Some of its landmarks carry the weight of wars and revolutions, while others whisper stories of dynasties, poets, and explorers. From ancient citadels to colonial-era relics, these sites tell the story of a country that has been shaped by power struggles, resilience, and a deep sense of cultural identity.

Hanoi, the capital, is a city where history feels alive. The Imperial Citadel of Thang Long stands as a testament to Vietnam's dynastic past. Once the seat of power for a thousand years, it's a place where emperors ruled, where war bunkers held secrets, and where archaeologists continue to unearth artifacts that date back centuries. The old stone gates and weathered walls may not be as imposing as they once were, but they hold the memory of a nation that has seen wars come and go. A short walk away, the Ho Chi Minh Mausoleum is a place of pilgrimage, where visitors pay their respects to the leader who reshaped Vietnam's future. His preserved body lies in state, watched over by solemn guards, while outside, the expansive Ba Dinh Square echoes with history—the very place where Ho Chi Minh declared Vietnam's independence in 1945.

In the heart of Hue, the Imperial City still carries the elegance of a bygone era. This walled fortress, once the stronghold of the Nguyen emperors, has endured war and time. Its palaces, pagodas, and lotus-filled ponds paint a picture of royal life, though many structures were destroyed during the battles of the 20th century. Walk through the grand Ngo Mon Gate, step into the Forbidden Purple City, and picture the lavish ceremonies that once took place here. At night, lanterns illuminate the ancient corridors, and the scent of incense lingers in the air. Not far from the citadel, the Royal Tombs of Hue lie scattered along the Perfume River. Each one reflects the personality of the emperor it was built for—some are modest, some are extravagant, but all are surrounded by serene gardens and poetic stone carvings.

Hoi An, a town that once thrived as a major trading port, has managed to hold onto its charm despite the passing centuries. The Japanese Covered Bridge, built by 16th-century merchants, still stretches over a quiet canal, its ornate carvings reflecting a time when Hoi An was a meeting place for traders from Japan, China, and Europe. Nearby, ancient assembly halls with dragon motifs and gilded altars tell the story of the Chinese communities who made this town their home. The entire Hoi An Ancient Town is a living museum, with centuries-old houses still standing along streets lit by colorful lanterns.

In the countryside outside Ninh Binh, the ruins of Hoa Lu, Vietnam's first capital, remain tucked between limestone mountains. This was the seat of power before Hanoi, where emperors ruled in the 10th and 11th centuries. Though little remains of the grand palaces, the ancient temples dedicated to King Dinh and King Le stand as reminders of Vietnam's earliest days as an independent kingdom. A short ride away, Bai Dinh Pagoda, the largest Buddhist complex in the country, feels both ancient and new, its massive bronze Buddha statues and towering stupas drawing pilgrims from across Vietnam.

Further south, Ho Chi Minh City is a city of contrasts, where colonial-era architecture stands beside modern skyscrapers. The Reunification Palace, frozen in time since 1975, is a symbol of the Vietnam War's end. Step inside, and it's like walking into a time capsule—telephones, radios, and maps left exactly as they were on the day Saigon fell. Outside, the streets pulse with energy, but inside, the underground bunkers and strategy rooms tell a different story. Nearby, the Saigon Notre-Dame Cathedral and the Central Post Office, both relics of French rule, add a European touch to the city's historic core.

Just outside the city, the Cu Chi Tunnels reveal the ingenuity and resilience of the Vietnamese during wartime. Crawling through these narrow underground passages, once used by the

Viet Cong, is a claustrophobic but eye-opening experience. This vast network of tunnels was a hidden world—an entire system of living quarters, kitchens, and trap-laden pathways that allowed resistance fighters to move undetected.

On the misty slopes of the northern mountains, Sapa's stone church stands as a quiet reminder of the French colonial presence in the region. Though small, the church has watched over the town for more than a century, a stark contrast to the surrounding rice terraces and traditional villages of the H'mong and Dao people. In the highlands of Tây Nguyên, the old Rong houses of the Bahnar and Jarai communities serve as cultural landmarks, their towering thatched roofs unlike anything else in Vietnam.

In the far south, Ba Chua Xu Temple in Chau Doc is more than just a place of worship—it's a spiritual landmark that draws thousands of devotees each year. Pilgrims climb Sam Mountain to make offerings to the "Lady of the Realm," a goddess believed to bring prosperity and protection. The atmosphere is a blend of faith and festivity, with incense swirling in the air and vendors selling trinkets and amulets.

Along the central coast, the ancient Cham Towers of Po Nagar in Nha Trang stand as remnants of a once-powerful Hindu kingdom. These red brick structures, built by the Champa civilization over a thousand years ago, are still places of worship, where locals burn incense and leave offerings to the goddess Yan Po Nagar. In Quy Nhon, the Tháp Đôi Cham Towers rise unexpectedly in the middle of the city, another reminder that long before the Vietnamese arrived, this land was home to another great culture.

Local Markets and Crafts

Vietnam's markets are where life happens. More than just places to shop, they are the heartbeat of communities, alive with the sounds of bargaining, the scent of fresh herbs, and the hum of daily routines. Whether in a bustling city or a quiet rural village, every market has its own rhythm. Some are centuries old, carrying traditions that haven't changed much over time, while others cater to modern tastes but still retain a sense of local identity. Beyond the stalls of fruit, spices, and textiles, these markets are also a window into Vietnam's craft heritage, where artisans continue skills passed down through generations.

In Hanoi, the Old Quarter's Dong Xuan Market is the city's largest and most chaotic. Vendors spill out onto the sidewalks, selling everything from dried squid to woven bamboo baskets. Inside, narrow aisles are crammed with fabric, electronics, household goods, and street food stalls dishing out steaming bowls of bún chả. Just a short walk away, Hang Gai Street, also known as Silk Street, is where you'll find tailor shops offering custom-made áo dài (Vietnam's traditional dress) and fine silk scarves. Many of these tailors source their silk from Van Phuc Village, just outside Hanoi, one of the country's oldest silk-weaving communities. The sound of looms still echoes through the village as artisans weave delicate patterns, continuing a craft that dates back over a thousand years.

In the southern metropolis of Ho Chi Minh City, Ben Thanh Market is a landmark in itself. The market has stood in various forms since the 19th century and remains one of the best places to experience the city's energy. In the early morning, local chefs and vendors stock up on fresh produce, while by afternoon, the market transforms into a tourist hub filled with souvenirs, handicrafts, and spices. For a more local experience, Cho Lon, the city's Chinatown, is home to Binh Tay Market, where the trade of dried goods, textiles, and traditional medicine still thrives. Walking through its maze of stalls, you'll catch glimpses of old shopfronts with hand-painted Chinese characters and the smell of roasted duck drifting from hidden alleyways.

In central Vietnam, Hoi An's Night Market is as much about atmosphere as it is about shopping. Lanterns hang overhead, casting a warm glow over stalls selling handwoven mats, ceramics, and hand-painted lanterns. The town itself has a long history of craftsmanship, and several villages nearby keep those traditions alive. Thanh Ha Pottery Village, just outside the town, has been producing ceramics for centuries. Walk through, and you'll see artisans shaping clay on foot-powered wheels, firing pots in traditional kilns, and carving intricate patterns into terracotta tiles. Nearby, Kim Bong Carpentry Village has been crafting wooden boats, furniture, and pagoda carvings since the 15th century. Many of Hoi An's most beautiful wooden buildings owe their decorative flourishes to the skills of these carpenters.

Hue, Vietnam's former imperial capital, is known for its delicate craft traditions. The city's Dong Ba Market carries everything from dried lotus seeds to conical hats, but the real treasures are found in the workshops outside the city. Tay Ho Village is where artisans still handcraft the iconic nón lá, the Vietnamese conical hat. Here, families sit together weaving palm leaves, using techniques that have remained unchanged for generations. Another Hue specialty is pháp lam, a form of enamelware that once adorned the walls of royal palaces. Though nearly lost, a few skilled artisans are reviving this craft, recreating intricate enamel panels and delicate jewelry.

In the far north, Bac Ha Market is the heart of trade for the ethnic minority groups of the region. Every Sunday, Hmong,

Tay, Dao, and Nung people travel from surrounding villages, dressed in their most colorful clothing, to trade livestock, handwoven textiles, and medicinal herbs. The market is a sensory overload—brightly embroidered skirts and blankets hang from wooden stalls, the scent of grilled buffalo meat fills the air, and traders bargain over baskets of chili peppers and mountain honey. The textiles here are works of art, with each pattern telling a story, passed down through generations of women who dye, weave, and embroider by hand.

In the Mekong Delta, the markets take to the water. Cai Rang Floating Market, near Can Tho, is the largest and liveliest. Before sunrise, wooden boats loaded with pineapples, jackfruits, and melons bob on the river, vendors calling out their prices as smaller boats weave through, selling bowls of noodle soup and Vietnamese coffee. Further south, in Chau Doc, Tan Chau Silk Village has been weaving silk for centuries. What sets it apart is its use of natural dyes, particularly the deep black silk dyed using Diospyros mollis fruit, a technique unique to the region.

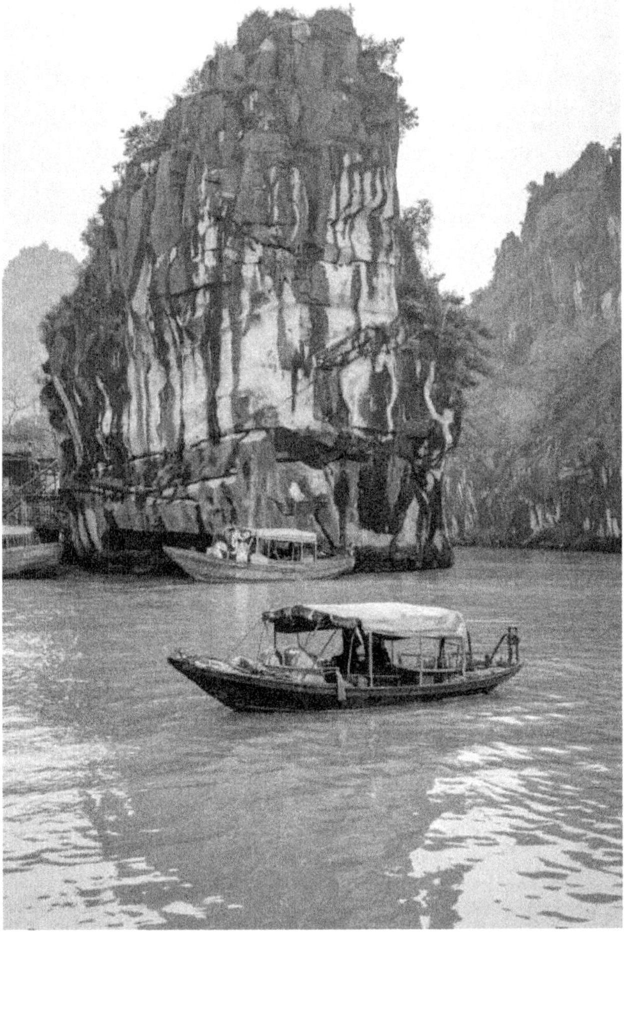

Culinary Delights

Vietnamese Dishes to Try

Vietnamese food is about balance—flavors, textures, and fresh ingredients all coming together in dishes that are light but deeply satisfying. Every region has its own take on the country's classics, and even the same dish can taste completely different depending on where you eat it. Whether it's a bowl of steaming noodles on a Hanoi street corner or a sizzling plate of seafood in the Mekong Delta, the best meals in Vietnam often come from the simplest places.

Phở is the dish that most people associate with Vietnam, and for good reason. This bowl of beef or chicken noodle soup is more than just comfort food—it's part of daily life. In Hanoi, where it originated, the broth is clear and intensely fragrant, simmered for hours with beef bones, star anise, and cinnamon. The noodles are flat and silky, and the toppings are kept simple—thin slices of beef, a handful of herbs, and maybe a squeeze of lime. Head south to Ho Chi Minh City, and the flavors get bolder. The broth is slightly sweeter, often served with hoisin sauce and chili paste on the side, along with a mountain of fresh herbs. Everyone has their favorite spot, from decades-old street vendors to hidden neighborhood eateries.

Bún chả is another Hanoi specialty that's impossible to ignore. Grilled pork patties and thin slices of caramelized pork belly are served in a bowl of sweet-savory fish sauce broth, with a plate of fresh herbs, rice noodles, and crispy spring rolls on the side. It's messy, flavorful, and best enjoyed at a roadside eatery with smoke rising from the charcoal grills. This was the dish that Anthony Bourdain and Barack Obama famously shared at a small shop in Hanoi, and it remains a local favorite.

Bánh mì is Vietnam's answer to the perfect sandwich. A crisp, airy baguette (thanks to the country's French colonial past) is stuffed with a mix of pâté, cured meats, pickled vegetables, fresh herbs, and chili. Variations exist across the country—Hoi An is famous for its version, with a secret sauce that soaks into the bread, while in Saigon, the fillings are more generous, sometimes including grilled pork, roast chicken, or even a fried egg.

Cao lầu is a dish you won't find outside of central Vietnam. This specialty from Hoi An is made with thick, chewy noodles that are said to be soaked in water from ancient Cham wells. The dish combines slices of pork, crunchy rice crackers, fresh herbs, and a light broth, creating a texture that's completely unique. Unlike phở or bún, this dish isn't about the soup—it's about the perfect mix of chewiness, crunch, and savory depth.

Mi Quang, another central Vietnamese noodle dish, is a bowl of wide rice noodles topped with shrimp, pork, herbs, peanuts, and a small amount of turmeric-infused broth. Unlike other noodle soups, this one isn't meant to be fully submerged in broth—it's more of a noodle salad with just enough liquid to bring everything together. It's a dish that feels both hearty and fresh at the same time.

Gỏi cuốn, or fresh spring rolls, are Vietnam's version of a light snack. These translucent rice paper rolls are packed with shrimp, pork, vermicelli noodles, and fresh herbs, served with a rich peanut dipping sauce or fish sauce-based dip. They're the opposite of the deep-fried spring rolls that many people are used to, but just as addictive.

Chả cá Lã Vọng is one of Hanoi's most famous dishes, and it's all about the experience. Turmeric-marinated fish is grilled and then finished in a sizzling pan at the table, where it's tossed with heaps of fresh dill and green onions. It's eaten with rice noodles, crushed peanuts, and fermented shrimp paste, creating a combination of flavors that's bold and slightly funky.

In the south, cơm tấm is a must-try. This "broken rice" dish is a staple in Ho Chi Minh City, served with grilled pork chops, pickled vegetables, a fried egg, and a drizzle of sweet-savory fish sauce. The name comes from the rice itself—fragments of grains that were once considered inferior but are now an essential part of the dish's texture.

Bánh xèo is Vietnam's take on a crispy, savory pancake. Made with rice flour and turmeric, it's stuffed with shrimp, pork, and bean sprouts, then folded like an omelet and eaten wrapped in lettuce leaves with fresh herbs. The key is dipping it in nước chấm, the fish sauce-based dipping sauce that balances sweet, sour, and salty flavors.

Huế, the former imperial capital, is home to bún bò Huế, a spicy, beefy noodle soup that's packed with lemongrass, chili oil, and tender slices of beef shank and pork. It's richer and bolder than phở, with a broth that has a deep, almost fiery complexity.

For something truly local, head to the Mekong Delta and try hủ tiếu, a noodle soup that varies from town to town. Some versions have a clear broth, while others are rich and porky. In Can Tho, you'll find hủ tiếu Nam Vang, a Cambodian-Vietnamese hybrid with ground pork, shrimp, quail eggs, and crispy fried garlic.

Desserts in Vietnam tend to be light and refreshing. Chè, a catch-all term for Vietnamese sweet soups, comes in endless varieties. Some are made with coconut milk, others with mung beans, jelly, or fruit. A favorite on hot days is chè ba màu, or "three-color dessert," a mix of red beans, pandan jelly, and sweetened coconut cream served over crushed ice.

Top Restaurants and Eateries

Vietnam's best meals aren't always found in fancy dining rooms. Some of the country's most unforgettable flavors come from tiny street stalls, decades-old family-run eateries, and local institutions that have perfected a single dish. Whether it's a no-frills noodle shop in Hanoi, a seafood shack by the beach, or a contemporary take on Vietnamese cuisine in Ho Chi Minh City, the best way to experience Vietnam is through its food.

In Hanoi, Pho Gia Truyen is the undisputed king of phở. This tiny shop on Bat Dan Street has been serving northern-style phở for generations, with a clear, deeply fragrant beef broth that simmers for hours. There are no extras here—just tender slices of beef, flat rice noodles, and a handful of green onions. It's no-nonsense, cash-only, and you might have to wait in line, but the first sip of broth makes it worth it. For something more communal, Bún Chả Hương Liên is the go-to spot for bún chả, the smoky, grilled pork dish that became internationally famous after Anthony Bourdain and Barack Obama ate there. The pork patties are served in a bowl of slightly sweet fish sauce broth, with fresh herbs and rice noodles on the side. Down the street, Banh Mi 25 is a favorite for Hanoi-style bánh mì, offering a crispy baguette stuffed with pâté, pork, pickled vegetables, and chili sauce.

Ho Chi Minh City has its own legendary food spots. Pho Hoa Pasteur is one of the city's oldest and most famous phở restaurants, serving a richer, slightly sweeter southern-style broth. A few streets away, Huynh Hoa is the heavyweight champion of bánh mì in Saigon. This sandwich is a monster—packed with layers of cold cuts, pâté, fresh cilantro, and pickled carrots, all stuffed inside a crackly baguette. If you're looking for something more contemporary, Anan Saigon, run by award-winning chef Peter Cuong Franklin, reinvents Vietnamese street food with a fine-dining twist. Located in the old wet market district, the menu features creative takes on classics, like a high-end bánh xèo and a caviar-topped bánh mì.

Hoi An is known for its local specialties, and Bánh Mì Phượng is the most famous sandwich shop in town. Anthony Bourdain called it the best bánh mì in the world, and the long lines outside suggest many agree. The secret is the house-made sauce that soaks into the bread, giving it an extra layer of flavor. For a sit-down meal, Morning Glory serves traditional Hoi An dishes in a more refined setting. The cao lầu, a noodle dish unique to the town, is a must-try. The chewy noodles, slices of roast pork, and crispy crackers all come together in a way that's completely different from other Vietnamese noodle dishes. For something more hands-on, Vy's Market Restaurant lets diners experience Hoi An's food culture through interactive cooking stations where you can watch (or try) traditional methods of making rice paper, dumplings, and more.

Hue, the former imperial capital, is home to some of Vietnam's most refined cuisine. Ba Do is a small family-run spot that specializes in bánh bèo, delicate steamed rice cakes topped with dried shrimp and crispy pork skin. Served in tiny dishes, they're meant to be eaten with a spoonful of sweetened fish sauce. Hanh Restaurant is another great choice, known for its wide variety of Hue specialties, including bún bò Huế, the city's famous spicy beef noodle soup. The broth here is deep, rich, and fragrant with lemongrass, and it's loaded with beef shank, pork hock, and cubes of congealed blood for those feeling adventurous.

Da Nang, known for its beaches and seafood, is the place to go for mi quang, a central Vietnamese noodle dish that's somewhere between a soup and a salad. Mi Quang Ba Mua is one of the most well-known places to try it, with turmeric-infused noodles, shrimp, pork, peanuts, and just a splash of broth. For seafood, Be Man is a local institution, where you pick your seafood from the tanks, and they prepare it however you like—grilled, steamed, or stir-fried with garlic and chili.

Nha Trang is all about fresh seafood, and Lac Canh is one of the city's most famous spots for grilled meats and seafood. The signature dish is beef marinated in a secret spice mix and grilled at the table over a charcoal fire. Bún Cá Lá Song is another must-visit, known for its bún chả cá, a noodle soup made with fish cakes, tomatoes, and a light but flavorful broth.

In the Mekong Delta, Can Tho's Cai Rang Floating Market is the best place to experience the region's food culture. Small boats weave through the market selling bowls of hủ tiếu, a noodle soup that comes in both a clear broth and a drier stir-fried version. On land, Sao Hom is a charming riverside restaurant that serves Mekong specialties like cá lóc nướng trui (grilled snakehead fish) and cơm cháy kho quẹt (crispy rice with caramelized fish sauce dip).

For those heading to Phu Quoc, the seafood shacks along Ham Ninh Fishing Village offer some of the freshest crab, shrimp, and squid you'll ever taste. For a more refined seafood experience, Gop Gio Restaurant is a local favorite, serving everything from grilled sea urchin to steamed grouper with ginger and soy.

Street Food and Night Markets

Vietnam's streets come alive at night. Neon signs flicker, the smell of grilled meat drifts through the air, and motorbikes weave through narrow alleyways as locals pull up plastic stools for an evening feast. Street food isn't just a way to eat—it's a way of life. The best meals in Vietnam often don't come from restaurants but from street vendors who have spent decades perfecting a single dish. From sizzling pancakes to steaming bowls of noodles, the country's night markets and street food stalls offer an experience that's as much about atmosphere as it is about taste.

Hanoi is the undisputed capital of street food. In the heart of the Old Quarter, Ta Hien Street comes alive after dark. This narrow stretch, often called "Beer Street," is packed with locals and travelers drinking bia hoi, Vietnam's signature draft beer, for as little as 10,000 VND a glass. The perfect pairing? Nem chua rán, deep-fried fermented pork rolls that are crispy on the outside and slightly tangy inside. A few streets away, Hang Buom Night Market is where you'll find vendors selling bánh gối, golden crescent-shaped pastries stuffed with minced pork, mushrooms, and vermicelli. Another must-visit is Dong Xuan Market, where you'll find bún riêu, a crab noodle soup with a rich, slightly tangy tomato-based broth, served with a plate of fresh herbs and chili.

Ho Chi Minh City's street food scene moves at a faster pace. Vinh Khanh Street in District 4 is the place to go for seafood. Every night, the street is packed with tables loaded with grilled octopus, tamarind crab, and clams cooked with lemongrass and chili. Vendors cook everything over open flames, sending bursts of fire into the air as they toss shrimp and squid onto red-hot grills. If you're in the mood for something different, Bui Vien Street in District 1 is famous for its fusion of local and international street food, from Vietnamese-style tacos to Korean-inspired barbecue skewers. But for something more traditional, head to Ben Thanh Street Food Market, where you'll find classics like bánh xèo, crispy rice pancakes filled with shrimp, pork, and bean sprouts, served with fresh lettuce and herbs for wrapping.

Hoi An's night market is as much about the atmosphere as it is about the food. Lanterns glow overhead, the river reflects the warm light, and vendors sell everything from silk lanterns to handmade jewelry. But the real highlight is the food stalls lining the market, where you can grab a bánh mì from the famous Madam Khanh - The Banh Mi Queen or sit down for a plate of cao lầu, Hoi An's signature noodle dish with thick chewy noodles, slices of pork, and crispy rice crackers. Another must-try is white rose dumplings, delicate steamed dumplings filled with shrimp and topped with crispy shallots.

Hue's street food is a little different—smaller portions, bold flavors, and a heavy influence from the imperial cuisine that once defined the city. Bánh bèo, steamed rice cakes topped with minced shrimp and crispy pork skin, are sold from tiny pushcarts along the Perfume River. Another Hue specialty is bún bò Huế, a spicy beef noodle soup with a deep, fragrant broth infused with lemongrass and chili. You'll find some of the best bowls at Ba Do, a tiny family-run spot that has been serving it for decades.

Da Nang's Helio Night Market is a favorite for both locals and visitors, with stalls selling grilled seafood, skewered meats, and regional specialties like mì Quảng, a turmeric-infused noodle dish topped with shrimp, pork, and crushed peanuts. The city's beaches also have their own informal night market scene, where seafood restaurants set up tanks of live fish, crabs, and shellfish, allowing diners to choose their meal before it's grilled to order.

Nha Trang, known for its seafood, has a night market that's packed with vendors selling fresh-off-the-boat delicacies. One of the best things to try is bò nướng lá lốt, minced beef wrapped in betel leaves and grilled over charcoal. The smoky, slightly peppery flavor pairs perfectly with a cold beer and a side of pickled vegetables. Another standout is bánh căn, small, crispy rice pancakes filled with shrimp or quail eggs, served with a tangy dipping sauce made from fish sauce, green mango, and fresh herbs.

In the Mekong Delta, Can Tho's Cai Rang Floating Market is an early-morning street food experience like no other. Vendors cook from their boats, serving steaming bowls of hủ tiếu, a noodle soup that's either served with a light broth or stir-fried with garlic and soy sauce. You'll also find bánh tét, a sticky rice cake wrapped in banana leaves, often sold in sweet or savory versions. At night, Can Tho's riverside night market is the best place to grab grilled banana sticky rice, a simple but delicious snack where sticky rice is wrapped around a banana, grilled until crispy, and served with coconut sauce.

Phu Quoc, known for its fish sauce and seafood, has one of the most exciting night markets in Vietnam. At Dinh Cau Night Market, you can find everything from grilled sea urchin topped with quail egg to bún kèn, a lesser-known but flavorful noodle soup made with minced fish, coconut milk, and lemongrass. The market also specializes in hải sản nướng, grilled seafood dishes like squid, prawns, and whole fish, all cooked fresh to order.

Cafés and Dessert Spots

Vietnam takes its coffee seriously. From tiny hole-in-the-wall cafés where old men sip cà phê sữa đá to trendy coffee shops experimenting with new brewing techniques, the café culture here is strong. Coffee isn't just a drink—it's part of daily life. The same can be said for Vietnam's desserts, which range from sweet soups to coconut-infused treats, best enjoyed at a street-side stall or a specialty dessert café. Whether you're in search of the perfect egg coffee, a refreshing bowl of chè, or a quiet spot to enjoy the buzz of the city, Vietnam has plenty of options.

Hanoi is the birthplace of cà phê trứng, or egg coffee, a thick, velvety concoction made by whipping egg yolks with sugar and condensed milk, then pouring it over strong Vietnamese coffee. The best place to try it is Café Giảng, a humble spot down a narrow alley where this famous drink was first created in the 1940s. It's rich, almost like a liquid tiramisu, and best enjoyed slowly. Another Hanoi institution is Cong Cà Phê, a chain known for its military-inspired décor and coconut coffee, a refreshing mix of coffee, coconut milk, and crushed ice. For something more modern, The Note Coffee near Hoan Kiem Lake is a charming little café covered in handwritten notes left by travelers from all over the world. The drinks are solid, but it's the atmosphere that makes it special.

Ho Chi Minh City has its own café scene, blending old-school coffee culture with a wave of hipster cafés. L'Usine is one of the city's most stylish spots, doubling as a boutique and café where you can sip a latte while browsing locally designed fashion and homeware. If you're after something more traditional, Cheo Leo Café is one of the oldest cà phê vợt (sock-filtered coffee) spots in the city, serving strong, smooth coffee made using a cloth filter—a technique that dates back nearly a century. For dessert, Maison Marou is a chocolate lover's paradise. This artisanal chocolate café, founded by the makers of Vietnam's famous Marou chocolate, serves rich single-origin hot chocolate, indulgent pastries, and handcrafted truffles.

Hoi An, with its lantern-lit streets and historic buildings, is home to some of the most atmospheric cafés in Vietnam. Reaching Out Tea House is a unique experience—this quiet, beautifully designed tea house is run by hearing-impaired staff, creating an environment of calm where guests communicate using wooden blocks and hand gestures. The tea and coffee are excellent, served in delicate handmade ceramics. If you're looking for a place to escape the heat, Rosie's Café is a cozy, modern spot tucked away in a quiet alley, known for its fresh juices, smoothie bowls, and strong Vietnamese coffee.

Hue, Vietnam's former imperial capital, has a more relaxed café culture, but there are still a few standout spots. Tan Café is one of the most well-loved in the city, serving rich, fragrant coffee with a side of history—its décor is filled with antiques and old photographs that reflect Hue's royal past. For something sweet, Hue is famous for chè, a broad category of Vietnamese desserts that include everything from sweetened beans and jellies to coconut-infused puddings. Chè Hem, a small, tucked-away dessert shop, serves some of the best variations, including chè bắp (sweet corn pudding) and chè hạt sen (lotus seed dessert).

Da Nang, a city known for its beaches and seafood, also has a growing café scene. 43 Factory Coffee Roaster is a must-visit for serious coffee lovers. This specialty coffee shop sources high-quality beans from around the world and brews them with precision, offering pour-over, espresso, and cold brew options in a sleek, minimalist setting. If you're in the mood for something sweet, Bánh Flan Đông Tịnh is a local favorite for bánh flan, Vietnam's take on crème caramel, served with crushed ice and strong black coffee for an extra kick.

Nha Trang, with its laid-back coastal vibe, has plenty of beachfront cafés where you can sip an iced coconut coffee while listening to the waves. An Café, set in a lush garden, serves some of the best coffee in town alongside traditional Vietnamese desserts like bánh bò (steamed rice cakes) and chè chuối (banana with coconut milk and tapioca pearls). For something a little different, Rainforest Café offers a jungle-like setting with hanging plants and treehouse-style seating, perfect for an afternoon coffee break.

In the Mekong Delta, the café culture is simpler but just as essential to daily life. Can Tho's Ninh Kieu Riverside Café offers a peaceful spot to enjoy a Vietnamese coffee while watching boats drift along the river. But for something truly local, nothing beats ordering a cà phê sữa đá from a floating vendor at Cai Rang Floating Market, where coffee is brewed on wooden boats and served in plastic cups as the market buzzes around you. For dessert, the Mekong Delta is home to some of Vietnam's best chè, with tropical flavors like durian, coconut, and pandan. Street stalls in Can Tho's night market sell bowls of chè thập cẩm, a mix of jellies, beans, and coconut milk served over crushed ice.

Phu Quoc, known for its beaches and seafood, has a few hidden café gems. Chuon Chuon Bistro & Bar sits on a hilltop, offering panoramic views of the island while you sip on a coconut coffee or a mango smoothie. For a sweet treat, Phu Quoc's Night Market is the place to go for grilled bananas drizzled with coconut sauce or kem trái dừa, coconut ice cream served inside a frozen coconut shell, often topped with roasted peanuts.

Food Festivals and Events

Food festivals and events are a highlight of Vietnam's vibrant culinary culture. The country's diverse regions each have their own food traditions, and these festivals celebrate the rich tapestry of flavors, dishes, and ingredients that define the Vietnamese table. From grand national events to small local celebrations, food festivals in Vietnam are not just about eating—they're a deep dive into the culture, history, and identity of each area.

The Hanoi Food Festival, usually held in October, is one of the largest and most popular food events in Vietnam. This festival showcases the best of Hanoi's culinary traditions, with street food stalls and pop-up restaurants offering local favorites like phở, bún chả, and cha ca. It's a time when the city's food scene comes together in one place, giving both

121

locals and visitors the chance to experience the full range of northern Vietnamese cuisine. The festival features cooking demonstrations, live music, and food contests, and it's an excellent opportunity to sample regional specialties from the far north, like thang cuốn (rice rolls) and bánh cuốn (steamed rice pancakes).

Tết Nguyên Đán, or Lunar New Year, is the most important food celebration in Vietnam. It's when families across the country prepare elaborate meals to honor ancestors and celebrate the arrival of the new year. The centerpiece of Tết cuisine is bánh chưng (a sticky rice cake wrapped in banana leaves), filled with mung beans and pork, symbolizing the Earth. Each region has its own variations of Tết food, but all meals are steeped in meaning and tradition. In major cities like Hanoi and Ho Chi Minh City, Tết markets spring to life with vendors selling everything from sweet treats like mứt (candied fruits) to fresh flowers, rice cakes, and ceremonial foods. These celebrations go beyond just feasting—they're about family, heritage, and welcoming new beginnings.

The Mid-Autumn Festival, or Tết Trung Thu, is another nationwide event that focuses on food and sweets. Held on the 15th day of the 8th lunar month, this festival celebrates the harvest moon and is particularly special for children. Lanterns fill the streets, and the centerpiece of the festival is mooncakes, a round pastry filled with lotus seed paste, red bean paste, or salted egg yolks. In cities like Hanoi and Ho Chi Minh City, mooncake markets appear, where artisans create beautifully decorated cakes, often with intricate designs and fillings. In addition to mooncakes, the streets come alive with snacks like chè (sweet soups) and bánh trung thu (snack cakes). This festival, while deeply tied to tradition, is also a celebration of family and community.

In the central region, Hue's Food Festival is a fantastic celebration of the imperial cuisine that once graced the royal courts. Held every two years, this event gathers chefs, food experts, and local food vendors to showcase the complex flavors of Huế's royal dishes. The food is sophisticated, often requiring hours of preparation. Highlights include bánh bèo (steamed rice cakes with shrimp), bún bò Huế (spicy beef noodle soup), and cơm hến (clam rice). The festival also features cooking classes, food exhibitions, and traditional music performances, making it a great way to understand how food and culture intertwine in Vietnam's imperial history.

The Ho Chi Minh City Street Food Festival celebrates the vibrant street food culture of the south. Held annually, this festival brings together local food vendors, restaurants, and food bloggers to showcase the best of Saigon's street food scene. The festival's outdoor setting allows visitors to wander through food stalls serving everything from bánh xèo (crispy rice pancakes) and hủ tiếu (noodle soup) to grilled meats and exotic fruit smoothies. Food trucks and street vendors add to the festival atmosphere, offering both traditional and fusion dishes. This event is a celebration of the region's culinary creativity and its ability to blend flavors from Vietnam's diverse food cultures.

In the Mekong Delta, Cai Rang Floating Market Festival is a food-focused event that honors the region's floating markets. Held in Can Tho, it's a festival that celebrates the food culture of the Mekong River, particularly its fresh produce and fish-based dishes. During the festival, the floating market itself becomes the venue for cooking competitions, food exhibitions, and tastings of local specialties like cá lóc nướng trui (grilled snakehead fish) and bánh xèo. The festival also features local music, dance, and traditional performances that bring the region's unique culture to life.

In Da Nang, the annual Da Nang International Food Festival attracts chefs from around the world to showcase global cuisine alongside Vietnamese specialties. This festival combines international flavors with traditional Vietnamese ingredients, offering a fusion of food that's as much about cultural exchange as it is about enjoying a meal. Alongside global chefs, local Vietnamese chefs display their mastery of dishes from the central region, like mì Quảng (turmeric noodles) and bánh canh (thick noodle soup). The festival is an excellent opportunity to explore Da Nang's local flavors and the diverse culinary influences that have shaped the city's food scene.

The Mekong Delta Food Festival, a newer addition to Vietnam's food calendar, is a celebration of the region's lush landscapes and rich agricultural produce. Held in Can Tho or other towns along the Mekong River, this festival highlights the importance of fresh, seasonal ingredients in Vietnamese cooking. The market features fruits like durian, mangoes, and rambutan, as well as fish and rice. Locally sourced dishes such as bánh tét (sticky rice cake), hủ tiếu, and regional variations of chè are served alongside cooking demonstrations and traditional music performances. The festival is a true celebration of the bounty of the Mekong River.

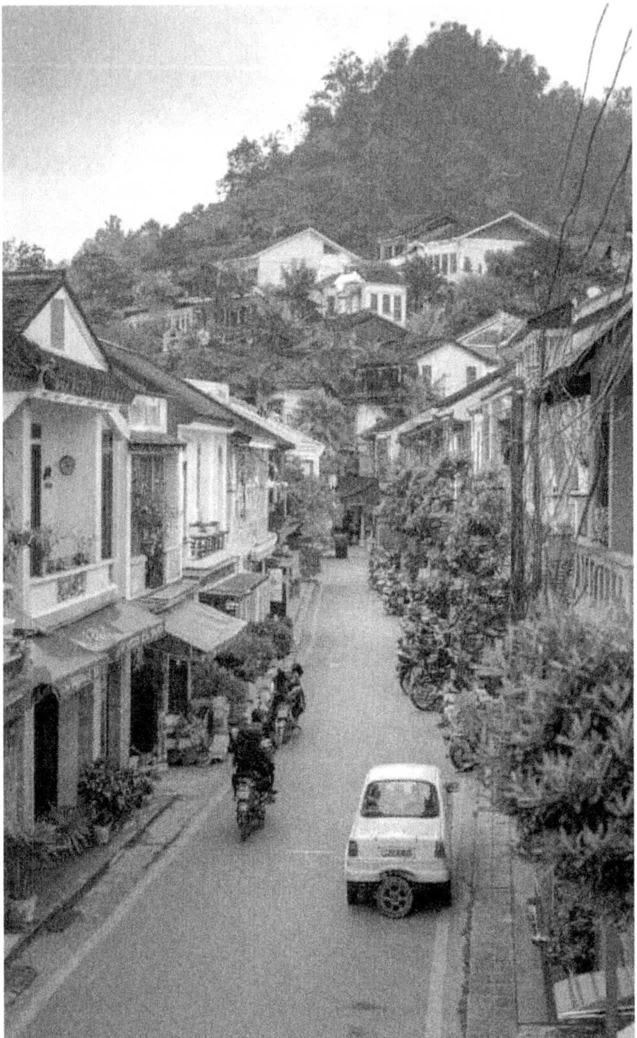

MUST SEE

Nightlife and Entertainment

Vietnam's nightlife and entertainment scene is as dynamic and diverse as the country itself. From vibrant night markets and late-night cafés to bustling bars, trendy clubs, and cultural performances, the options are endless. Whether you're in the mood to enjoy live music, sip cocktails on a rooftop bar, or experience traditional dance and theater, Vietnam offers something for every taste and every time of night.

In Hanoi, the nightlife is centered around the Old Quarter, where the streets pulse with activity long after the sun sets. Ta Hien Street, known as "Beer Street," is the perfect place for an evening out, with street vendors serving up ice-cold bia hơi (Vietnamese draft beer) alongside salty snacks. The atmosphere is casual, with a mix of locals and travelers gathered at low plastic tables to drink and chat. For something a bit more laid-back, head to Bia Zakka, a popular local bar with a relaxed vibe, where you can sip on craft beer and enjoy a game of darts or pool. If you're after something more upscale, The Rooftop Bar offers stunning views of the Hoan Kiem Lake and Hanoi's skyline, making it a great spot for a cocktail at sunset.

In Ho Chi Minh City, the nightlife is fast-paced and cosmopolitan. Bui Vien Street in District 1, often referred to as the city's "Backpacker Street," is where the action is. This lively street is packed with bars, clubs, and street food vendors, and it's where both locals and tourists gather to party into the early hours. For a more refined experience, head to the Bitexco Tower's Sky Deck, where you can sip cocktails while taking in panoramic views of the city. The Deck in District 2 offers a more tranquil setting, perfect for dinner by the river, followed by a drink as the city lights twinkle across the water. If you're looking for a clubbing scene, Lush and Envy are two of the city's most popular nightclubs, attracting a young, energetic crowd with live DJ sets and dance floors.

Hoi An, known for its historic charm, also has a growing nightlife scene. The town's nightlife is more low-key compared to the hustle and bustle of Hanoi or Ho Chi Minh City, but it's still lively and full of character. After the lanterns light up the streets in the evening, head to Dive Bar, a laid-back venue popular with both locals and expats. The bar hosts regular live music performances and is a great spot to enjoy a cold beer and chat with other travelers. If you're in the mood for something more energetic, Q-Bar offers a chic setting with cocktails, music, and dancing in the heart of the Ancient Town.

In the coastal city of Da Nang, the nightlife revolves around its beach resorts and bars with sea views. The Rooftop Bar at Vanda Hotel offers sweeping views of the ocean, and is one of the best places in the city to watch the sunset with a drink in hand. For a more local experience, Bamboo2 Bar is known for its relaxed vibe, serving drinks and playing reggae music. Da Nang also has a thriving karaoke scene, with private rooms available in many bars and clubs, where locals gather to belt out their favorite songs until the early morning hours.

Nha Trang, a beach town on the central coast, is known for its laid-back yet lively nightlife. Sailing Club is one of the best spots in the city to party by the beach, with live DJ performances and beachside cocktails. For a more chill vibe, head to Louisiane Brewhouse, a beachfront bar and brewery where you can sample local craft beers while watching the waves. If you're in the mood for a night out with dancing, Khai Hoan Nightclub is one of the city's most popular clubs, drawing in a mix of locals and tourists with its electric atmosphere.

Hue, the former imperial capital, offers a more refined nightlife scene, with a focus on cultural entertainment. One of the most unique experiences in Hue is attending a Royal Theatre Performance at the Imperial Palace. This traditional performance, featuring court music, dance, and historical reenactments, gives visitors a glimpse into the grandeur of the Nguyen Dynasty. If you prefer a more relaxed evening, DMZ Bar is a popular spot for live music, while The Brown Eyes Bar has a cozy ambiance, perfect for sipping cocktails and enjoying the night air.

In the Mekong Delta, the town of Can Tho has a vibrant riverside nightlife. Ninh Kieu Wharf is the focal point of the city's nightlife, with many cafes, bars, and restaurants lining the river. Take a boat ride at sunset, followed by dinner at one of the riverside restaurants offering fresh seafood. The Lounge Bar in Can Tho is another great spot for a drink, often featuring live music and an easygoing atmosphere. The night markets in Can Tho also come alive after dark, offering local delicacies and a chance to immerse yourself in the local culture.

Phu Quoc, Vietnam's largest island, has a laid-back yet lively nightlife scene centered around its beautiful beaches. O'Club Beach Bar is a popular spot, offering music, cocktails, and a chance to unwind on the sand while watching the sunset. Shenron Lounge provides an elegant atmosphere with delicious cocktails and views of the sea. For a more local experience, Dinh Cau Night Market offers food stalls, live music, and street food, making it an ideal place to enjoy the warm evening air while snacking on grilled seafood or bánh mì.

Day Trips and Excursions

Vietnam is a country of contrasts, where bustling cities, peaceful rural landscapes, and stunning natural beauty are all just a short journey apart. Day trips and excursions are a fantastic way to explore beyond the main tourist spots, offering the chance to experience local culture, outdoor adventure, and Vietnam's diverse landscapes. Whether you're seeking history, nature, or a bit of both, Vietnam's day trips offer something for every kind of traveler.

From Hanoi, a day trip to Ninh Binh is a must for those who want to experience the country's stunning karst landscape without the crowds of Ha Long Bay. Known as "Halong Bay on land," Ninh Binh is filled with towering limestone cliffs, lush rice paddies, and tranquil rivers. Take a boat ride through Tam Coc, passing through caves and green fields, or visit the Trang An Scenic Landscape Complex, a UNESCO World Heritage site. For a more active excursion, hike to the top of Mua Cave for panoramic views of the surrounding countryside.

For a history-filled day trip, head to Hoa Lu, Vietnam's ancient capital before it was moved to Hanoi. The site is home to temples dedicated to the Dinh and Le dynasties, set against a backdrop of stunning limestone mountains. The serene environment offers a glimpse into Vietnam's early history and is a peaceful alternative to the more crowded tourist spots around Hanoi.

From Ho Chi Minh City, one of the most popular day trips is to Cu Chi Tunnels, located about 30 kilometers outside the city. This extensive network of underground tunnels was used by the Viet Cong during the Vietnam War and offers a fascinating, if humbling, look at the resilience and resourcefulness of the soldiers. You can crawl through the tunnels, visit the kitchens, and learn about the strategies that were employed during the war.

For a day trip immersed in natural beauty, head to Mekong Delta. The region, known for its network of rivers, canals, and floating markets, is a wonderful way to experience rural Vietnam. Take a boat ride through the maze of waterways, stop at small riverside villages, and explore the floating market at Cai Be or Cai Rang. You can also visit local workshops to see how coconut candy, rice paper, and traditional Vietnamese conical hats are made. The lush scenery, tranquil atmosphere, and vibrant markets make this a memorable excursion.

If you're staying in Da Nang, a visit to the Marble Mountains offers an easy yet rewarding day trip. These five limestone hills, located just outside the city, are filled with caves, pagodas, and shrines, and offer panoramic views of the coastline. For a cultural experience, explore the Buddhist altars and temples tucked within the caves or climb to the top for a stunning view of Da Nang and the surrounding countryside. It's a peaceful retreat, just a short drive from the bustling city.

In Hoi An, a day trip to My Son Sanctuary is a fascinating exploration of Vietnam's ancient Cham civilization. Located about 40 kilometers from Hoi An, this UNESCO World Heritage site features a series of Hindu temples and towers that date back to the 4th century. Set in a lush green valley, the temples offer insight into the religious and architectural practices of the Cham people. The site is less crowded than other ancient landmarks in Vietnam, providing a tranquil setting for history enthusiasts.

Hue is another city surrounded by a wealth of day trip options. A visit to Thien Mu Pagoda, located on the banks of the Perfume River, offers a combination of history and natural beauty. The seven-story pagoda is one of the oldest and most iconic structures in Vietnam, and it offers a peaceful escape from the city. For a bit of adventure, take a boat ride along the river to reach the pagoda, and enjoy the beautiful scenery along the way.

If you're in Nha Trang, take a boat trip out to the nearby Vinpearl Island, a popular day excursion known for its beaches, an amusement park, and a large aquarium. You can access the island via the longest cable car ride in the world, offering stunning views of Nha Trang Bay. Once on the island, you can relax on the beach, visit the water park, or explore the underwater world at the aquarium.

For a truly unique experience, a day trip to Phu Quoc offers the chance to explore pristine beaches, visit fishing villages, and enjoy the fresh seafood the island is known for. You can also take a boat trip to the nearby An Thoi Archipelago and spend the day snorkeling, swimming, or simply enjoying the island's untouched natural beauty. Dinh Cau Night Market in the evening provides a lively atmosphere, where you can try local delicacies and shop for handmade souvenirs.

In Sapa, you can embark on a trek through the terraced rice fields of the Muong Hoa Valley. A day hike will lead you through picturesque villages, where you can meet local ethnic minority groups like the H'mong and the Tay, and witness their traditional way of life. If you're looking for a more relaxed day, head to Fansipan Mountain, the highest peak in Vietnam. You can either hike to the top or take the cable car for an easy ride to the summit, where you'll be rewarded with panoramic views of the surrounding valleys and mountains.

Lastly, Phan Thiet offers a fantastic beach day trip with a cultural twist. Visit the Mui Ne Sand Dunes, where you can take a thrilling ride on a sandboard or simply marvel at the shifting golden sands. The dunes are especially beautiful at sunrise or sunset, making it a perfect spot for photography. Afterwards, enjoy a day by the beach, known for its warm waters and good conditions for windsurfing.

Family-Friendly Activities

Vietnam offers a wide range of family-friendly activities that cater to all ages, from exploring vibrant cities to relaxing in nature, and experiencing the country's rich culture. The diversity of landscapes, historical landmarks, and entertainment options makes it easy for families to find something fun and educational for everyone. Whether you're looking for outdoor adventures, interactive museums, or unique cultural experiences, Vietnam has plenty to keep children and parents alike entertained.

In Hanoi, the Vietnam Museum of Ethnology is an excellent spot for families to learn about the country's diverse cultures in a fun and interactive way. The museum features exhibits on the 54 ethnic groups of Vietnam, with colorful displays of traditional costumes, artifacts, and models of traditional houses. The outdoor area, with its life-size replicas of ethnic homes, allows children to run around while learning about the architectural styles of different communities. The museum's hands-on exhibits and engaging storytelling make it a great educational stop.

For an outdoor adventure, take a family-friendly day trip to Ba Vi National Park, located just outside Hanoi. The park offers scenic hikes, picnic spots, and plenty of opportunities to enjoy nature. The Tay Con Linh Range is ideal for an easy family hike, and you'll be rewarded with stunning views of the surrounding landscape. The park also has attractions like the King's Temple and a bamboo forest, making it a peaceful and fun escape from the hustle and bustle of Hanoi.

In Ho Chi Minh City, families can enjoy a variety of indoor and outdoor activities. The Saigon Zoo and Botanical Gardens is one of the oldest zoos in Vietnam and is perfect for children who love animals. The zoo has a wide range of animals, including elephants, tigers, and monkeys, as well as lush gardens where you can relax. It's a great way for kids to learn about wildlife while enjoying some time outdoors.

Another great family activity in Ho Chi Minh City is a visit to the Saigon Skydeck at the Bitexco Tower, where families can enjoy panoramic views of the city from the 49th floor. The observation deck is interactive, with information about the city's history and future development, making it a fun and educational experience. Kids will love spotting famous landmarks from the height, and there's a café at the top to enjoy a drink with a view.

If you're in Hoi An, a great family activity is taking a lantern-making workshop. Hoi An is famous for its colorful lanterns, and many local shops offer hands-on workshops where families can learn to make their own. Children can get creative while learning about this traditional craft, and they'll leave with a souvenir they made themselves. The workshops are typically short and engaging, making them a perfect family-friendly activity.

For a bit of adventure, head to the Hoi An Water Puppet Theatre, where families can watch a traditional Vietnamese water puppet performance. This type of theater is a unique form of storytelling, where puppets float on water and enact scenes from Vietnamese folklore and rural life. The bright colors, music, and lively performances make it a great show for children.

In Da Nang, families can take a trip to Ba Na Hills and ride the world's longest cable car to the top of the mountain. Once there, you'll find The Golden Bridge, a stunning pedestrian bridge held up by two giant stone hands. It's an impressive sight, and there are plenty of activities at the summit, including an amusement park, a giant indoor amusement area, and gardens for children to explore.

For a more relaxed day, head to My Khe Beach in Da Nang. The beach is known for its clean sands and calm waters, making it a great spot for families to swim, build sandcastles, or simply relax under the sun. There are many beachfront cafes where you can enjoy a meal with a view.

In Nha Trang, the Vinpearl Land Amusement Park is a fantastic destination for families. This large park is located on Vinpearl Island and offers a mix of attractions, including an aquarium, water park, and theme park rides. The park also has a large outdoor area where families can enjoy a range of activities, from water slides to roller coasters. You can reach the park via the cable car, which offers breathtaking views of the ocean and surrounding islands.

For a more nature-focused activity, the Nha Trang National Oceanographic Museum is a fun and educational visit for families interested in marine life. The museum showcases a variety of sea creatures and marine ecosystems, with interactive exhibits that kids can engage with. It's both entertaining and informative for all ages.

In Phu Quoc, families can enjoy the laid-back atmosphere while exploring the island's natural beauty. Vinpearl Safari is a large wildlife park where you can take a safari tour to see animals in their natural habitats. The park also offers a variety of interactive activities for children, including petting zoos and play areas. For a relaxing day by the beach, Long Beach is a family-friendly spot with calm waters where kids can safely swim or try their hand at paddleboarding.

If you're in Sapa, take a scenic trek through the rice terraces and local villages. Sapa is famous for its terraced rice fields, and there are easy walks suitable for families that offer a chance to interact with local ethnic minority communities. The Cat Cat Village is a popular stop, where you can learn about the traditional culture of the H'mong people, watch handicraft demonstrations, and enjoy a peaceful stroll through the countryside. Children will love the opportunity to meet local kids and see how they live in the stunning mountain landscape.

For a more immersive experience, take a boat trip around Hoan Kiem Lake in Hanoi. The calm waters and picturesque surroundings make it a peaceful spot for families to relax. You can also rent bicycles or explore the nearby parks and gardens for a family outing that combines nature with a touch of local culture.

Hidden Gems

Vietnam is a country of well-known landmarks and popular tourist destinations, but it's also home to countless hidden gems waiting to be discovered. These lesser-known spots offer a more authentic, off-the-beaten-path experience, allowing travelers to see a different side of the country, away from the crowds. From remote villages and untouched beaches to lesser-explored islands and secret temples, these hidden gems offer tranquility, beauty, and a glimpse into Vietnam's rich history and culture.

In the northern mountains, the small town of Bac Ha in Lao Cai Province is a true hidden gem. Known for its colorful weekly market, Bac Ha is home to the Flower H'mong people, and the market is a riot of color, with locals selling everything from intricate textiles to fresh produce. The town is surrounded by lush valleys, steep hillsides, and vibrant flower fields, making it a picturesque and peaceful place to visit. For a true escape, head to the nearby Hoàng Su Phì, famous for its terraced rice fields that stretch across the mountains, offering breathtaking views and an incredible opportunity to experience rural life in northern Vietnam.

Further north, the Ban Gioc Waterfall, located on the border between Vietnam and China, is one of the most spectacular and least-visited waterfalls in the country. Surrounded by limestone karsts and lush forests, this hidden gem is a serene spot for nature lovers and photographers. You can take a boat ride to get closer to the falls or simply admire the view from the banks of the river. It's a peaceful and remote location, far from the usual tourist crowds, making it a perfect spot for those looking to connect with nature.

In central Vietnam, the Phong Nha-Kẻ Bàng National Park is home to some of the most stunning caves in the world, but it remains a hidden gem for many travelers. While the famous Son Doong Cave gets much of the attention, Phong Nha Cave and Tien Son Cave are just as impressive and much more accessible. These caves feature intricate rock formations, underground rivers, and stunning stalactites and stalagmites. Phong Nha is also home to lush jungles, rivers, and waterfalls, offering ample opportunities for hiking, kayaking, and exploring off-the-beaten-path landscapes.

For those interested in history, the Quang Tri Province near the border with Laos is home to the Vinh Moc Tunnels, a lesser-known alternative to the Cu Chi Tunnels. These tunnels were used by local villagers during the Vietnam War to protect themselves from bombings. The tunnels are a fascinating and sobering insight into the resilience of the people in the face of war. Quang Tri is also home to the DMZ (Demilitarized

Zone), where you can visit the Ben Hai River and La Vang Holy Land, a historical site with a mix of Catholic and local influences.

In Hoi An, while the ancient town is well-known, An Bang Beach is a hidden gem that offers a more peaceful and relaxed atmosphere than the often-crowded Cua Dai Beach. This stretch of sand is less developed and more natural, with calm waters and fewer tourists, making it a great place to relax. There are also small local restaurants along the beach where you can enjoy fresh seafood while watching the sunset.

In Da Nang, Son Tra Peninsula is a tranquil and underrated spot for nature lovers. The peninsula, also known as the "Monkey Mountain," offers lush forests, pristine beaches, and scenic viewpoints, including the iconic Lady Buddha statue, which is one of the tallest statues in Vietnam. The area is home to a variety of wildlife, including the endangered red-shanked douc langur, a species of monkey native to the region. For a peaceful retreat away from the city, this is the perfect hidden gem.

Down in the Mekong Delta, Ben Tre Province is an often-overlooked destination that offers a more authentic experience of the delta. While places like Can Tho get much of the attention, Ben Tre is quieter, with its lush coconut groves, tranquil waterways, and friendly locals. You can explore the area by boat, visit local workshops where traditional crafts like coconut candy are made, and experience the unique lifestyle of the people who live along the delta's waterways.

For beach lovers, the island of Con Dao, located off the southern coast of Vietnam, is one of the best-kept secrets in the country. Known for its pristine beaches, crystal-clear waters, and diverse marine life, Con Dao is a hidden paradise that remains relatively untouched by mass tourism. The island is also home to the Con Dao National Park, where you can hike, snorkel, or simply relax by the beach. The island has a dark history as a former prison during the French colonial period, and you can visit the Con Dao Prison to learn about its past.

Further south, Phu Quoc Island is well-known for its beaches, but the island's Vinpearl Safari is a hidden gem worth exploring. This wildlife sanctuary is home to a variety of animals, including rare species such as giraffes, zebras, and tigers. The safari is an ideal spot for families and nature lovers who want to experience wildlife in a more serene and intimate setting, without the crowds of more commercialized zoos.

For a unique cultural experience, head to The Cham Islands off the coast of Hoi An. These islands are home to the Cham people, an ancient civilization that once controlled much of central Vietnam. The islands are less touristy than nearby destinations and offer a glimpse into the Cham people's traditional way of life. You can visit Bai Xep Beach to relax and swim, or take a boat ride to explore the nearby Lang Beach and enjoy some of the freshest seafood you'll ever taste.

Finally, for an authentic and serene retreat, the Bac Son Valley in the northeast is a hidden gem surrounded by dramatic limestone mountains and lush rice fields. It's the perfect place for trekking and experiencing traditional village life, where you can meet the Tay, H'mong, and Dzao people. The valley is remote, which means fewer tourists, and it offers one of the best views of rural Vietnam's stunning beauty.

Accommodation Options

Luxury Hotels

In Vietnam, the landscape of luxury hotels is as diverse and impressive as the country itself, offering everything from opulent city-center retreats to serene beachside escapes. The country's luxury hotel scene combines modern elegance with traditional Vietnamese charm, creating a perfect blend of comfort and cultural experience.

In Hanoi, Sofitel Legend Metropole Hanoi stands out as one of the city's most iconic luxury hotels, located at 15 Ngo Quyen Street in the French Quarter. This elegant hotel is steeped in history and was established in 1901. The French colonial architecture exudes grandeur, while the modern amenities cater to the most discerning guests. The hotel offers a range of rooms and suites with luxurious furnishings and expansive city views. Prices for a standard room start at approximately 4,000,000 VND per night, with suites costing significantly more. The hotel features several dining options, including the famous Le Beaulieu, a French restaurant with a reputation for exquisite fine dining. Open 24/7, guests can also enjoy the spa, the outdoor pool, or afternoon tea in the historical setting of the hotel's grand lobby. The Metropole is just a short walk from major attractions like Hoan Kiem Lake and the Old Quarter.

In Ho Chi Minh City, The Reverie Saigon is a luxury experience that will leave guests in awe. Situated on the 27th to 39th floors of the Times Square building at 22-36 Nguyen Hue Boulevard, this hotel redefines opulence with its Venetian-inspired design, world-class service, and panoramic views of the city. Rooms start at 6,000,000 VND per night, with suites ranging higher. Guests can enjoy luxury dining at The Royal Pavilion, which serves authentic Cantonese cuisine, or relax by the pool with views of the Saigon River. The hotel's The Spa offers a serene escape, providing traditional therapies and contemporary wellness treatments. If you're after a truly indulgent experience, the hotel also boasts a private shopping gallery, perfect for high-end retail therapy.

In Da Nang, InterContinental Danang Sun Peninsula Resort is one of the country's most remarkable luxury beach resorts, located at Bai Bac, Son Tra Peninsula. Built into the mountainside, the resort offers stunning views of the ocean and has a unique blend of modern design and Vietnamese cultural elements. The property features lavish villas and suites starting at approximately 7,000,000 VND per night. The resort offers an incredible range of activities for guests, from private yacht excursions to yoga and spa treatments. For dining, the resort boasts several upscale restaurants, including La Maison 1888, which offers fine French cuisine with a Vietnamese twist. The resort also offers easy access to Son Tra Nature Reserve, a natural paradise with lush forests, wildlife, and hiking trails. The resort's private beach, pools, and spa make it the perfect destination for those seeking both relaxation and adventure.

For a more intimate retreat in Hoi An, The Nam Hai is one of Vietnam's premier luxury resorts. Located along the coast of Ha My Beach, just a short distance from the UNESCO World Heritage-listed Old Town, this resort is known for its minimalist luxury and exceptional service. Rooms start around 6,000,000 VND per night. The resort's stunning villas feature private pools, panoramic views of the beach, and lush tropical gardens. For dining, The Beach Restaurant offers fresh seafood and international dishes, while The Bar serves handcrafted cocktails in an elegant setting. Guests can also enjoy the resort's wellness programs at the spa or spend the day exploring Hoi An's ancient town. The Nam Hai's tranquil atmosphere makes it perfect for families or couples seeking a private and luxurious experience away from the crowds.

In Nha Trang, The Anam is one of the most luxurious resorts in Vietnam, located at Bai Dai Beach, Cam Ranh. It offers a colonial-style design with wide beachfront views and a focus on providing exceptional service. Rooms start at 3,000,000 VND per night, and the resort has a range of suites and villas. With a beautiful beach, two large pools, and several fine dining options, the resort is perfect for those looking to unwind in style. The Anam Restaurant offers gourmet Vietnamese cuisine, while The Beach Bar serves fresh cocktails by the ocean. Families can take advantage of the kid-friendly amenities, including a children's pool and a range of activities for younger guests.

In Phu Quoc, JW Marriott Phu Quoc Emerald Bay Resort & Spa stands out as an incredibly luxurious escape, located on the island's stunning southern coastline. This resort offers an experience steeped in both natural beauty and exquisite design, with each room starting at 5,500,000 VND per night. The resort's design, inspired by the story of an ancient university, is quirky and elegant, with vibrant colors, lavish furnishings, and a fantastic beach setting. Guests can dine at The Pink Pearl, an upscale French restaurant, or unwind at one of the many beachside bars. The resort offers an array of activities, including a stunning spa, watersports, and an infinity pool overlooking the beach. For a truly indulgent experience, guests can book a private villa or indulge in a bespoke spa treatment designed for ultimate relaxation.

Lastly, Sofitel Legend Metropole Hanoi, The Reverie Saigon, InterContinental Danang Sun Peninsula Resort, The Nam Hai, and JW Marriott Phu Quoc Emerald Bay Resort & Spa are just a few examples of the exceptional range of luxury hotels that can be found throughout Vietnam. With their exceptional service, remarkable architecture, and world-class amenities, these properties offer an unforgettable experience for those seeking both relaxation and adventure in a country that blends the old and the new.

Budget Hotels and Hostels

In Vietnam, budget hotels and hostels offer a variety of options for travelers seeking affordable yet comfortable accommodations. Whether you're a backpacker exploring the country's vibrant cities or simply looking to save on lodging, these spots provide excellent value without compromising on quality or location. From bustling cities like Hanoi and Ho Chi Minh City to beach destinations like Da Nang and Phu Quoc, budget-friendly accommodations are widely available.

In Hanoi, Hanoi Backpackers Hostel at 9 Ma May Street is one of the most popular spots for budget-conscious travelers. A lively, sociable atmosphere and close proximity to the Old Quarter make it a favorite among backpackers. Rooms range from dorms to private rooms, with prices starting at approximately 200,000 VND per night for a dorm bed. The hostel features a rooftop bar where guests can mingle with fellow travelers, along with an in-house restaurant serving both Vietnamese and Western food. Check-in is available 24/7, and the staff is always ready to offer recommendations for activities in Hanoi. The hostel's central location makes it easy to explore nearby attractions like Hoan Kiem Lake, the Night Market, and the Temple of Literature.

Another great option in Hanoi is The Little Hanoi Hostel, located at 45 Bat Dan Street, right in the heart of the Old Quarter. This budget hotel offers clean, no-frills rooms starting at around 300,000 VND per night. Despite its affordable price, the hotel provides exceptional service and is known for its friendly and welcoming staff. It's a solid choice for travelers who need a basic, comfortable place to rest after a day of sightseeing. Guests can enjoy free Wi-Fi, breakfast, and the convenience of being within walking distance to popular sites such as the Hoan Kiem Lake and Hanoi's bustling markets.

In Ho Chi Minh City, The Saigon Hostel at 213 De Tham Street in District 1 is a popular choice for budget travelers. Offering a range of rooms from shared dorms to private options, prices start at about 250,000 VND per night for a bed in a dorm. The location is ideal for those wanting to explore the city's vibrant nightlife, markets, and food scene, as it's just a short walk from Bui Vien Street. The hostel has a relaxed and friendly atmosphere, with communal spaces where guests can socialize. It also offers organized tours, which is convenient for those looking to explore more of the city or take day trips.

For those seeking a hostel with a slightly more upscale feel, The Hideout Hostel at 311/15 Pham Ngu Lao Street offers a cozy space with prices starting at 300,000 VND per night for a bed in a shared dorm. The atmosphere is laid-back, with modern decor, a rooftop bar, and an inviting common area. Its location in the heart of District 1 means you're within easy reach of attractions such as the Ben Thanh Market, Notre Dame Cathedral, and the War Remnants Museum. The staff at The Hideout Hostel are known for their helpfulness, offering great local tips and making sure you feel at home.

In Da Nang, Funtastic Hostel on 73 Hoang Hoa Tham Street is an excellent choice for budget-conscious travelers looking for comfort without the hefty price tag. Starting at 200,000 VND for a dorm bed, this hostel offers a clean, friendly environment with easy access to the city's attractions. It's a short distance from My Khe Beach, where you can relax on the sand or take part in water sports. The hostel also has a common area, a kitchen for self-catering, and a bar where you can meet other travelers. The staff here are great at organizing tours to nearby attractions like the Marble Mountains and Ba Na Hills.

For travelers visiting Phu Quoc, Langchia Hostel at 117 Tran Hung Dao is a budget-friendly accommodation option with private rooms starting at around 350,000 VND per night. Phu Quoc is famous for its pristine beaches, and Langchia Hostel's convenient location makes it easy to explore the island's beauty without breaking the bank. The rooms are simple but comfortable, and the hostel offers free Wi-Fi and breakfast, along with a relaxed atmosphere that's perfect for those looking to unwind after a day of beach activities.

In Hoi An, Hoi An Backpackers Hostel at 14 Nguyen Duy Hieu Street is a great budget accommodation located near the historic Old Town. Prices start at about 150,000 VND per night for a dorm bed. This vibrant, social hostel is perfect for those who enjoy meeting other travelers and being part of a lively atmosphere. It has a large swimming pool, a bar, and plenty of organized activities like pub crawls and walking tours to explore Hoi An's historic sites and famous lantern-lit streets. The hostel also offers rental bikes, allowing guests to easily explore the countryside and nearby beaches.

For those looking for a quiet, no-frills place to rest in Hue, Hue Backpackers Hostel at 23 Nguyen Tri Phuong Street is an excellent choice. Prices start around 200,000 VND per night for a dorm bed, and the hostel offers a mix of shared and private rooms. The friendly staff are knowledgeable about the city's rich history, and they often organize group outings to visit the Imperial City, Thien Mu Pagoda, and the ancient tombs of Hue's emperors. The hostel provides free Wi-Fi, a communal kitchen, and a cozy lounge area for relaxing after a day of sightseeing.

Nha Trang, known for its beaches and laid-back vibe, offers budget-friendly options like Nha Trang Beach Hostel located at 47/1 Tran Phu Street. Starting at 250,000 VND per night for a dorm bed, the hostel is a short walk from the beach, making it a perfect choice for those looking to enjoy both the sea and the city. The common areas are well-kept, and there's a bar to enjoy a drink in the evenings. Guests can rent bikes and explore the city, or take part in daily activities such as beach volleyball, yoga classes, and sightseeing tours.

Boutique Hotels and Homestays

In Vietnam, boutique hotels and homestays provide travelers with the opportunity to experience the country's charm in more intimate and personalized settings. These accommodations often combine modern comforts with traditional Vietnamese elements, offering a welcoming atmosphere that allows guests to feel at home while enjoying the country's unique culture. Whether you're in a bustling city, near the beach, or exploring historic towns, Vietnam's boutique hotels and homestays offer an exceptional way to stay.

In Hanoi, The Hanoi Club Hotel & Lake Palais Residences, located at 76 Yen Phu Street, offers a luxurious and stylish stay with a scenic view of West Lake. Prices for rooms begin around 1,800,000 VND per night. The hotel blends French colonial architecture with modern amenities, creating a comfortable yet historical atmosphere. Guests can enjoy a range of services, including a spa, outdoor pool, and a restaurant serving both local and international dishes. Its central location makes it easy to explore the surrounding areas like the Old Quarter, Hoan Kiem Lake, and nearby historical landmarks.

For something more intimate, Cottage House at 17 Ma May Street offers a homestay experience with a boutique feel. Prices start at about 700,000 VND per night. It combines traditional Vietnamese decor with modern touches, offering a cozy retreat from the bustling city. The owners are known for their personal service, providing helpful local tips and offering homemade breakfast to guests. The homestay's location allows for easy access to Hanoi's famous attractions like Hoan Kiem Lake and the surrounding Old Quarter.

In Ho Chi Minh City, The Myst Dong Khoi, located at 6-8 Ho Huan Nghiep Street in District 1, offers an elegant blend of modern design and traditional Vietnamese influences. Prices for rooms start around 3,000,000 VND per night. The boutique hotel features luxurious amenities, including a rooftop pool, restaurant, and bar with panoramic views of the city. Its prime location allows guests to explore nearby attractions such as the Saigon Opera House and Ben Thanh Market with ease.

For a homestay experience, Saigon Oi Homestay at 107/9 Hoang Hoa Tham Street provides a warm and welcoming atmosphere, with room rates starting at 600,000 VND per night. It offers a more local, personalized stay where guests can enjoy home-cooked meals, connect with the hosts, and receive useful recommendations for exploring the city.

Though a bit off the main tourist path, the homestay is still close enough to major attractions, such as the War Remnants Museum and the Reunification Palace, making it a perfect spot for travelers who want a more authentic experience.

In Da Nang, Little Flower Boutique Hotel, located at 73 Hoang Hoa Tham Street, offers stylish and affordable accommodations with room prices starting at around 900,000 VND per night. The hotel's location provides easy access to Da Nang's beaches and landmarks like the Marble Mountains. The charming atmosphere and personalized service make it a great place for those looking for a quiet, relaxing retreat with modern amenities.

For a more intimate homestay, Hoang Anh Homestay provides a cozy, local feel with rooms starting from 800,000 VND per night. Located near Da Nang's city center, it offers a comfortable stay with a friendly, family-oriented atmosphere. Guests can explore the city, take part in local activities, or simply relax in the peaceful setting of the homestay.

In Hoi An, Little Riverside Hoi An offers a serene escape along the Thu Bon River, with prices starting at 1,500,000 VND per night. This boutique hotel blends traditional and modern design, providing an elegant atmosphere with views of the river and a relaxing pool. The hotel's location makes it easy to explore Hoi An's UNESCO-listed Old Town, with its vibrant lantern-lit streets and historical architecture. For a more personalized experience, Hoi An Garden Villas offers a homestay option starting at 800,000 VND per night. It's a peaceful retreat set within beautiful gardens, offering a family-like atmosphere while still being close to the Old Town.

In Hue, La Residence Hotel & Spa combines French colonial elegance with modern luxury. Located at 5 Le Loi Street, room prices start at 2,500,000 VND per night. The hotel's classic design and premium amenities, including a spa, rooftop bar, and restaurant, make it an ideal choice for those looking to explore Hue's historical sites. Guests can easily visit the Imperial City, Thien Mu Pagoda, and the ancient tombs of Hue's emperors. Alternatively, Phong Lan Homestay offers a more intimate experience with rooms starting at 600,000 VND per night. The hosts provide warm hospitality and homemade meals, allowing guests to immerse themselves in the local way of life while staying near Hue's famous landmarks.

In Nha Trang, Mojzo Inn Boutique Hotel at 8A Nguyen Thi Minh Khai Street offers a comfortable, stylish stay starting at 1,200,000 VND per night. This boutique hotel provides a cozy atmosphere with personalized service and easy access to Nha

Trang's beach. Guests can relax by the beach or enjoy the hotel's restaurant and bar. For a more homey experience, Nha Trang Homestay provides simple accommodations starting at 500,000 VND per night, offering a local touch with delicious homemade meals and a quiet retreat from the city.

For those visiting Phu Quoc, The Green Bay Phu Quoc Resort & Spa offers a boutique hotel experience right by the beach, with prices starting at 3,000,000 VND per night. With its tranquil setting, stunning views, and luxurious amenities, the resort offers the perfect balance of relaxation and adventure. Guests can also indulge in the in-house restaurant and explore nearby natural attractions. Alternatively, Coco Palm Beach Resort offers a homestay experience with a starting price of 800,000 VND per night. Set close to the beach, it combines affordability with comfort, providing a more intimate experience with local charm.

Beach Resorts and Eco-Lodges

Vietnam's coastline is lined with stunning beaches and lush landscapes, making it the perfect destination for beach resorts and eco-lodges. These places offer more than just beautiful views—they provide a chance to relax, unwind, and connect with nature in settings that often emphasize sustainability, local culture, and luxury. Whether you're looking for a serene beachside retreat or an eco-conscious hideaway, Vietnam has options that cater to all kinds of travelers, blending comfort and environmental respect.

On Phu Quoc Island, Coco Palm Beach Resort is a standout for those seeking an eco-friendly getaway. Located along Bai Khem Beach, the resort offers an immersive tropical experience with spacious bungalows and private villas that start at approximately 1,500,000 VND per night. It's a haven for those looking to enjoy nature while minimizing their carbon footprint. The resort uses sustainable practices in its operations, including the use of solar energy, organic gardening, and eco-friendly materials in the construction of its buildings. Guests can enjoy the beautiful beach, relax by the pool, or take part in water sports like kayaking and snorkeling. For those interested in local culture, the resort offers tours to explore Phu Quoc's fishing villages and the famous Vinpearl Safari.

In Da Nang, InterContinental Danang Sun Peninsula Resort is one of the most luxurious eco-resorts in the country, with rooms starting at 5,500,000 VND per night. Situated on the Son Tra Peninsula, this resort offers stunning views of the ocean and a commitment to sustainability through practices like waste reduction and sourcing local products. The resort's blend of modern luxury and nature provides a unique experience, with spacious villas, an infinity pool, and several dining options offering organic, locally-sourced ingredients. The resort also offers eco-tours in the nearby Son Tra Nature Reserve, where visitors can explore the lush forests and observe the diverse wildlife of the area.

For a more low-key yet equally charming stay, The Nam Hai in Hoi An is an ideal eco-lodge and resort that offers beachfront villas starting at around 4,500,000 VND per night. The resort sits on a pristine stretch of sand, surrounded by tranquil gardens and the soft breeze of the South China Sea. The Nam Hai emphasizes sustainable luxury, with its design incorporating local materials and natural elements. The on-site spa focuses on wellness using organic products, and the resort has an organic garden to supply fresh ingredients for the restaurant. Guests can enjoy beach yoga, cooking classes, or simply relax by the pool or the beach. Hoi An's UNESCO-listed Old Town is nearby, offering a chance to explore traditional Vietnamese architecture and vibrant local markets.

For a truly off-the-beaten-path experience, Six Senses Ninh Van Bay in Nha Trang is an eco-resort that allows you to disconnect and rejuvenate. Located in a secluded bay, this resort offers villas starting at around 8,000,000 VND per night, all with spectacular views of the ocean. The eco-resort blends into its surroundings with a focus on environmental sustainability, using natural materials and energy-efficient systems throughout the property. The resort's activities are designed to immerse you in nature, with kayaking, diving, and hiking, while the spa offers organic treatments to soothe and rejuvenate. For a truly immersive experience, guests can participate in environmental preservation activities, such as coral reef restoration or turtle monitoring programs. The untouched nature of Ninh Van Bay offers a tranquil setting for anyone looking for a peaceful retreat.

In Mui Ne, The Sailing Club Resort is a more affordable option for those seeking a beachfront escape with eco-conscious practices. Prices start around 2,500,000 VND per night. The resort offers a range of bungalows and villas with stunning ocean views, all designed to blend seamlessly with the natural landscape. The eco-resort focuses on sustainability, promoting green tourism through practices like using locally sourced food, reducing plastic waste, and maintaining an organic garden. Guests can relax by the beach, enjoy windsurfing, or unwind at the resort's wellness center, which offers yoga and meditation classes. The resort's beachfront bar and restaurant serve fresh, locally sourced seafood and cocktails.

In Con Dao, Six Senses Con Dao is an exclusive eco-luxury resort that offers seclusion and sustainable living on a private island. Prices start around 10,000,000 VND per night. The resort's luxurious villas, some with private pools, offer breathtaking views of the sea and are designed with natural, sustainable materials. The Six Senses brand is known for its focus on environmental conservation, and the Con Dao resort is no exception. The property runs on solar power, maintains an organic farm, and participates in marine conservation efforts, including sea turtle protection programs. Guests can take part in eco-activities, from snorkeling in pristine coral reefs to hiking the island's trails. The resort's on-site spa and wellness center provide holistic treatments using organic products, ensuring that guests enjoy both luxury and a connection to nature.

On Bai Xep Beach in Phu Yen Province, Hoa Mai Homestay offers a more intimate eco-lodge experience. Prices start around 600,000 VND per night for a room. This homestay is located just steps from the beach and is run by a local family that focuses on sustainability and community. The homestay provides a cozy and laid-back atmosphere, offering organic, home-cooked meals using ingredients from the farm. Guests can enjoy various activities like beachcombing, cycling, or exploring nearby fishing villages. The focus here is on preserving the natural environment and supporting the local community, making it an ideal option for those looking for a genuine eco-lodge experience.

Unique and Unusual Stays

Vietnam offers some truly unique and unusual stays that go beyond the standard hotel experience, providing travelers with a chance to immerse themselves in the country's rich culture and natural beauty in unexpected ways. Whether you're looking for a stay in a floating house, a traditional wooden stilt house, or a modern design hidden in the jungle, Vietnam has no shortage of creative and unforgettable accommodations that will make your trip even more memorable.

In Ha Long Bay, staying on a traditional wooden boat is a must for those looking for a truly unique experience. Bhaya Cruises offers overnight cruises on the iconic emerald waters of Ha Long Bay, with rooms starting at around 2,500,000

VND per night. The boat is designed with traditional Vietnamese style and modern comforts, featuring luxurious rooms with panoramic sea views. The experience includes swimming, kayaking, and exploring some of the bay's lesser-known caves and floating fishing villages. At night, guests can relax on deck under the stars, making it a peaceful and unforgettable escape on the water.

For something even more unusual, head to Ninh Binh, where you can stay in a treehouse at Ninh Binh Hidden Charm Resort, located in a lush valley near the stunning Trang An Scenic Landscape Complex. Prices for treehouse stays begin at about 1,500,000 VND per night. Set amidst nature, these treehouses provide an immersive experience with panoramic views of the surrounding mountains and rice paddies. You'll feel completely connected to nature while enjoying modern amenities in an eco-friendly environment. The resort also offers tours of the nearby caves, temples, and picturesque rivers, making it a great base for outdoor adventures.

In Sapa, a stay in a traditional stilt house is a fantastic way to experience the local culture of the ethnic minority groups who live in the region. Sapa Eco-Lodge offers stays in these wooden stilt houses, with prices starting around 1,200,000 VND per night. Located in the Muong Hoa Valley, this eco-lodge provides guests with a chance to interact with local

H'mong, Tay, and Dao people, learning about their traditions, crafts, and farming practices. The homestay experience allows you to live alongside the villagers, sharing meals, participating in activities, and enjoying breathtaking views of terraced rice fields and the surrounding mountains.

For something entirely off the grid, Phu Quoc offers La Veranda Resort, a quirky and unique stay inspired by French colonial architecture, set on the pristine shores of Long Beach. With prices starting at around 4,500,000 VND per night, the resort offers an atmosphere full of vintage charm and old-world elegance, making it a perfect retreat for those looking for a romantic getaway with a historic touch. While not a typical "unusual" stay, the architecture and ambiance make it feel as if you've stepped into another time, offering a unique escape with all the modern comforts of a luxury resort.

In Hoi An, The Hoi An Historic Hotel is a traditional Vietnamese mansion with a story to tell, combining modern design with the charm of a historic property. The hotel offers suites that allow guests to enjoy the unique feeling of staying in a traditional Vietnamese house with the luxury of modern amenities. Prices for rooms start at approximately 2,000,000 VND per night. The hotel is conveniently located in the center of Hoi An's Ancient Town, a UNESCO World Heritage site, giving guests easy access to the city's markets, temples, and lantern-lit streets.

For those seeking a truly boutique homestay experience, La Vie En Rose Homestay in Phong Nha offers something entirely different. Situated in a peaceful village near Phong Nha-Kẻ Bàng National Park, the homestay features colorful rooms and a garden full of roses and lush greenery. Prices for stays here start at 800,000 VND per night. The owners, a local family, welcome guests into their home, providing a warm, friendly atmosphere. You can experience local life, take part in cooking classes, and explore the nearby caves and natural wonders that the area is famous for.

If you're seeking an artistic stay, the The House of The Gods in Da Nang is a stylish and unusual design hotel that feels like an art gallery. Prices for rooms start at about 2,000,000 VND per night. The hotel features modern, minimalist designs with unique artworks scattered throughout the property, creating an artistic and peaceful atmosphere. It's located near My Khe Beach, offering a perfect combination of design and natural beauty for those who appreciate creativity in their surroundings.

In Hue, The Ancient Hue Garden Houses offer a distinctive experience of staying in traditional Vietnamese garden houses with an emphasis on the architecture and culture of the Nguyen dynasty. The accommodations start at around 1,500,000 VND per night. These houses feature private courtyards, intricate wooden furniture, and beautiful gardens, providing a blend of culture and luxury. Guests can explore the ancient Imperial City of Hue and enjoy the traditional atmosphere of these historical homes.

For an eco-friendly twist on a beach vacation, The Nature Lodge in Mui Ne offers an off-the-grid experience with eco-lodges made from bamboo and reclaimed materials, starting at around 1,000,000 VND per night. Nestled on the edge of the desert and surrounded by sand dunes, the lodge provides a tranquil escape from city life, with a focus on sustainability. Guests can enjoy kite surfing, explore the famous sand dunes, or relax by the beach, knowing their stay is having minimal impact on the environment.

If you're after a glamping experience in Ninh Binh, Cuc Phuong National Park offers an incredible opportunity to sleep under the stars in luxury tents. Located in the heart of Vietnam's oldest national park, the glamping experience begins at approximately 1,200,000 VND per night. Guests can explore the surrounding forest, hike to waterfalls, and visit the nearby primate rescue center, all while staying in a comfortable and eco-friendly tent equipped with everything you need for a luxurious outdoor experience.

Practical Information

Currency and Banking

When traveling in Vietnam, understanding the currency and banking system is key to navigating daily expenses with ease. The official currency is the Vietnamese Dong (VND), and it's widely accepted throughout the country. As of now, 1 USD is worth approximately 23,000 VND, though the exchange rate can fluctuate. You'll find most prices listed in Vietnamese Dong, and it's helpful to have a basic understanding of how the currency looks and feels.

You'll typically come across bills in denominations of 10,000, 20,000, 50,000, 100,000, and 500,000 VND, with coins being relatively rare. The bills are colorful, and the higher the denomination, the larger and more ornate they tend to be. In terms of cash, larger notes are often used for bigger transactions, while smaller ones are useful for day-to-day purchases like food, transport, or souvenirs.

ATMs are widely available in cities and larger towns, so withdrawing cash is not difficult, but it's important to note that many ATMs charge a transaction fee, typically ranging from 30,000 to 50,000 VND per withdrawal. While ATMs offer the convenience of getting cash as you need it, keep in mind that some rural areas may not have easy access to ATMs, so it's a good idea to carry enough cash if you're heading to more remote regions.

For paying bills or purchases, most larger establishments like hotels, restaurants, and shops in major cities accept credit cards (Visa, MasterCard, and sometimes American Express). However, it's common practice to pay in cash at smaller local businesses, especially in places like street markets or small eateries. Card payments may also incur additional fees depending on the merchant. Foreign cards are accepted in major cities, but smaller towns and rural areas may not be as card-friendly.

If you prefer to exchange money, there are plenty of currency exchange services available at airports, banks, and exchange kiosks in tourist areas. However, the rates at airports tend to be less favorable, so it's usually better to change money in the city or use an ATM. Money changers in tourist-heavy areas are an option, but it's important to ensure the exchange rates are fair and the transactions are legitimate.

Most banks in Vietnam offer standard banking hours from 8 AM to 5 PM, Monday through Friday, with some branches open on Saturdays for a shorter period. It's easy to find a bank branch or ATM in larger cities, and if you need assistance, most banks will have English-speaking staff available. While many businesses accept foreign currency, it's best to have local currency on hand, as small transactions are rarely conducted in anything but VND.

Finally, tipping isn't mandatory, but it is appreciated. Small tips for services like taxi rides, hotel staff, or tour guides are common, and rounding up the bill is a nice gesture in many places. In general, tips of 10,000 to 20,000 VND are a reasonable amount, though you can adjust based on the service provided.

Language Tips and Communication

When traveling through Vietnam, getting a good grasp of the local language and communication customs can enhance your experience, helping you connect with locals and navigate your way around more easily. Vietnamese is the official language, and while many people in major cities and tourist areas can speak some English, especially in hotels or restaurants, it's still useful to learn a few basic phrases in Vietnamese to show respect for the culture.

One of the most important things to know is how to greet people. "Xin chào" (pronounced "sin chow") is a friendly, general greeting that works in most situations. To say "thank you," the word "Cảm ơn" (pronounced "kahm un") is commonly used, and "Vâng" (pronounced "vung") means "yes," while "Không" (pronounced "kohng") means "no." Simple pleasantries like these will go a long way, especially in more rural areas, where a little effort to speak the language is often met with smiles.

The Vietnamese language can be tricky due to its six tones, which can change the meaning of words depending on how they're pronounced. For example, "ma" can mean "ghost," "but," or "rice seedling" depending on the tone. This can be confusing at first, but don't worry too much—locals will appreciate any attempt to speak their language, even if your pronunciation isn't perfect.

In the larger cities and tourist spots, many young people can communicate in English, particularly at hotels, restaurants, and in the service industry. However, it's important to keep in mind that the level of English proficiency may vary. In more rural areas or small towns, fewer people may speak English, so having a translation app or phrasebook handy can be very useful.

In general, the Vietnamese are known for their politeness, so when engaging in conversation, it's a good idea to be respectful and considerate. Using titles like "ông" (for older men) and "bà" (for older women) is a polite way to address someone. For example, "ông chủ" would be used for a male shopkeeper or restaurant owner. While not necessary in every interaction, it can help convey respect.

When asking for directions, most locals will be happy to assist, but they may not always have a perfect understanding of English. It's often best to use simple phrases, and it helps to know a few key words for directions like "trái" (left), "phải" (right), and "thẳng" (straight). If in doubt, pointing at a map or showing your destination written down in Vietnamese can help clarify things.

Tipping in Vietnam is not mandatory, but it's appreciated, especially in more tourist-centric areas. If you're satisfied with the service, a small tip of about 10,000 to 20,000 VND is a nice gesture. Taxi drivers, hotel staff, and tour guides typically expect a small tip as well.

For more serious communication needs, having a translation app on your phone can make life much easier. Google Translate has become a widely used tool for both written and spoken translation, and many locals are familiar with it. You can even take a picture of menus or signs for instant translation, which can be incredibly helpful in non-touristy areas.

Health and Medical Services

When traveling in Vietnam, it's important to be aware of the health and medical services available, as they can vary significantly depending on where you are. In major cities like Hanoi, Ho Chi Minh City, and Da Nang, medical care is generally good, with a mix of public and private hospitals and clinics offering a range of services. For basic medical needs, such as minor injuries, illnesses, or routine check-ups, you'll find plenty of well-equipped facilities. Many of these hospitals have English-speaking staff, which can be helpful if you're not fluent in Vietnamese.

In Hanoi, hospitals like Hanoi French Hospital or Vinmec International Hospital provide high-quality care, with modern facilities and experienced doctors. These private hospitals cater to both locals and expats, offering everything from general health consultations to specialist treatments. Emergency services are also available at these locations, and while the cost is higher than at public hospitals, the level of service is typically more streamlined and comfortable. Prices at private hospitals may range from 500,000 VND for a consultation to several million for more complex treatments, depending on the type of service you need.

In Ho Chi Minh City, FV Hospital and Family Medical Practice are two prominent private healthcare providers that cater to foreign visitors. These hospitals are known for their Western-trained doctors, modern equipment, and a more comfortable environment compared to public facilities. While medical care in these private institutions is generally excellent, it can be costly, so travel insurance that covers medical expenses is strongly recommended for visitors.

Public hospitals in Vietnam, such as Bach Mai Hospital in Hanoi or Cho Ray Hospital in Ho Chi Minh City, offer a more affordable option. While they are often crowded and may not have English-speaking staff on hand, the treatment is still competent. For more serious health issues, you may be directed to larger hospitals or specialists, but be prepared for potentially longer wait times and less personalized care compared to private hospitals. If you're traveling in more remote areas, medical services may be more limited, and traveling to a larger city for care may be necessary if an emergency arises.

Pharmacies are widespread throughout Vietnam, and many are open late into the evening, especially in tourist areas. Most pharmacies will stock common medications like painkillers, antibiotics, and cold remedies. It's a good idea to bring a basic first aid kit with you, especially if you have specific medical needs or prescriptions. If you need something more specialized, the staff at pharmacies are usually able to direct you to the appropriate treatment, or you can visit a local doctor or clinic.

In terms of preventive care, vaccinations are an important consideration when visiting Vietnam. It's recommended to check with a healthcare provider before your trip to ensure you are up to date on routine vaccines like hepatitis A and B, typhoid, and tetanus. Malaria is a concern in some rural areas, particularly in the central and northern parts of the country, so it's advisable to take precautions against mosquito bites, such as using insect repellent and sleeping under nets. Dengue fever is also present, so it's best to take precautions when traveling in areas with a high risk of mosquitoes.

Safety Tips

Vietnam is a beautiful and welcoming country, but like any destination, it's important to stay mindful of your surroundings and take basic precautions to ensure a safe and enjoyable trip. With its bustling cities, scenic landscapes, and vibrant culture, Vietnam offers countless opportunities for exploration, but a few safety tips can help you avoid any potential hassles along the way.

When navigating the streets, especially in Hanoi and Ho Chi Minh City, be aware of the traffic. The traffic can feel chaotic, especially with the constant flow of motorbikes weaving through the streets. Always use crosswalks where available and try to cross at designated pedestrian crossings. When crossing the road, move steadily and confidently; traffic will often adjust to your pace. It might feel intimidating at first, but with a bit of practice, you'll get the hang of it.

As a general rule, keep your personal belongings secure. Petty theft can happen, particularly in crowded areas or on public transportation. It's a good idea to use a money belt or a secure bag with zippers to keep your valuables safe. If you're carrying a backpack, consider using a lock or keeping it in front of you in crowded places. Avoid displaying expensive jewelry or gadgets that might attract unwanted attention.

When it comes to money, always use reputable exchange services. At airports or major tourist spots, the exchange rates can sometimes be less favorable. Try to withdraw cash from ATMs at banks, as they're generally safer than those in convenience stores or tourist areas. Be cautious about exchanging money with street vendors, as scams can occasionally occur.

In terms of food and water safety, stick to bottled water and avoid drinking from tap water, as it may lead to stomach issues. Make sure the seal on the water bottle is intact before purchasing. When it comes to food, street food in Vietnam is part of the culture and can be delicious, but use your judgment. Choose food from busy stalls with high turnover, as these tend to be fresher. If you're unsure about the cleanliness of a place, opt for restaurants or eateries that seem to have a higher standard of hygiene.

Vietnam is generally a safe country for solo travelers and tourists, but always exercise caution when it comes to nighttime safety. While violent crime is rare, petty crime and scams are more common. Avoid walking alone in poorly lit or isolated areas, especially late at night. If you're in a new area, take a taxi or use a reputable ride-hailing service like Grab to get around after dark.

When engaging in water-based activities, especially in places like Phu Quoc or Da Nang, always follow safety guidelines provided by operators. Ensure that the equipment is in good condition, and if you're not confident in your swimming abilities, consider wearing a life jacket, even if it's not mandatory. Also, pay attention to weather conditions, as Vietnam's coastal regions can experience strong currents during certain seasons.

Natural disasters like floods, typhoons, or heavy rain can occur, particularly during the monsoon season, which runs from May to October. If you're traveling during these months, be sure to check weather reports frequently. In case of severe weather, follow local authorities' instructions and be prepared to adjust your plans if needed.

When booking tours or hiring guides, it's best to choose reputable operators who have positive reviews and proper licenses. Whether it's a day tour to Ha Long Bay or a trekking expedition in Sapa, make sure the company you choose follows all safety protocols, including proper equipment and trained guides.

For those exploring remote areas or trekking in places like Phong Nha-Kẻ Bàng National Park, always inform someone about your plans, especially if you're going off the beaten path. Carry a phone with local SIM cards or ensure you have a GPS device if venturing into isolated regions. Having a first-aid kit on hand can also help with minor injuries or accidents during more adventurous activities.

Scan the QR code to view full Vietnam map